Relational Database Management: Design, Transactions, and Monitoring

James Relington

DEDICATION

To those who seek knowledge, inspiration, and new perspectives—
may this book be a companion on your journey, a spark for curiosity,
and a reminder that every page turned is a step toward discovery.

Relational Database Management: Overview and Evolution 8

Fundamentals of Relational Databases.....................................11

Database Models and Their Role in Design.............................14

Relational Database Design: An Introduction.........................18

Normalization: The Key to Effective Database Design 21

Entity-Relationship Modeling in Database Design 25

Constraints in Relational Databases: Types and Importance.............28

Data Integrity and Validation in Relational Databases.....................32

Introduction to SQL: The Language of Relational Databases..............35

Querying Relational Databases with SQL.............................38

Advanced SQL Queries and Functions.................................42

Transaction Management in Relational Databases...........................46

ACID Properties: Ensuring Transaction Reliability...........................49

Concurrency Control: Managing Simultaneous Transactions.............52

Database Locks and Their Impact on Transactions 56

Isolation Levels and Their Influence on Database Operations 59

Rollbacks and Recovery Mechanisms in Relational Databases 63

Relational Database Indexing: A Performance Booster 66

Types of Indexes and Their Use Cases.................................70

Joins and Their Role in Relational Database Queries.........................73

Subqueries: Nested Queries for Complex Data Retrieval 77

Data Redundancy and How to Avoid It in Database Design..............80

Optimizing SQL Queries for Better Performance 83

Database Partitioning: Managing Large Data Sets 87

Relational Database Storage: Tables, Files, and Pages.....................91

Backups and Restores: Safeguarding Database Integrity....................94

Database Monitoring: Why It's Essential..............................98

Real-Time Database Monitoring Tools...............................101

Database Performance Tuning: Techniques and Best Practices........105

Database Security: Protecting Data and Access....................109

User Authentication and Authorization in Relational Databases 112

Auditing and Compliance in Relational Database Management........116

Replication in Relational Databases: Benefits and Challenges 120

High Availability and Disaster Recovery in Databases 123

Cloud Databases: Relational Databases in the Cloud 127

Distributed Databases: Challenges and Solutions...............................131

Database Scaling: Vertical and Horizontal Approaches 135

Data Warehousing and Relational Databases 138

Data Migration: Moving Data Across Different Databases 142

Data Modeling: Best Practices for Effective Database Design............145

Database Views: Simplifying Complex Queries 149

Materialized Views: Improving Query Performance...........................152

Triggers: Automating Actions in Relational Databases......................156

Stored Procedures: Enhancing Database Logic..................................159

Functions and Their Use in Database Design.....................................163

The Role of Metadata in Relational Databases....................................166

Data Aggregation and Reporting in Relational Databases 170

Relational Databases and Big Data: An Integration Approach...........173

Artificial Intelligence and Machine Learning in Relational Databases
....177

Future Trends in Relational Database Management Systems 181

Best Practices for Maintaining and Managing Relational Databases 185

AKNOWLEDGEMENTS

I would like to express my deepest gratitude to everyone who contributed to the creation of this book. To my colleagues and mentors, your insights and expertise have been invaluable. A special thank you to my family and friends for their unwavering support and encouragement throughout this journey.

Relational Database Management: Overview and Evolution

Relational Database Management Systems (RDBMS) are the backbone of modern data storage and management practices. They allow organizations to store, retrieve, and manipulate data efficiently in a structured and organized manner. The evolution of RDBMS began in the late 1960s and early 1970s when computer scientists recognized the need for a more effective and flexible way of handling data compared to the hierarchical and network models that were in use at the time. The relational model was first introduced by Edgar F. Codd, a researcher at IBM, in 1970. His revolutionary idea was based on set theory and formal logic, where data could be stored in tables with rows and columns, making it easier to manage and query. This was a departure from the complex hierarchical structures that were common in earlier systems.

In the early days of RDBMS, data was often managed by proprietary systems, which were complex and difficult to scale. As demand for more powerful and scalable systems grew, the relational model gained traction. One of the key features of relational databases is their ability to represent data in a way that is independent of its physical storage. This means that the structure of the data, or the schema, can be designed without worrying about the underlying hardware or storage mechanisms. This abstraction allowed organizations to focus more on the logical structure of their data and how it should be organized and queried rather than on the technical details of storage.

The early implementations of RDBMS were largely theoretical. They were not widely adopted until the 1980s, when commercial database systems began to emerge. IBM's DB2, Oracle, and Microsoft SQL Server were among the first to provide practical implementations of the relational model. These systems allowed organizations to manage vast amounts of data more efficiently and reliably, and they offered a variety of features that helped streamline database administration. One of the most significant advancements during this period was the introduction of Structured Query Language (SQL), a standardized programming language used to manage and manipulate relational databases. SQL made it easier for users to interact with databases without needing to understand the underlying complexities of the system. SQL became the de facto language for relational databases and continues to be widely used today.

As the 1990s progressed, the complexity of databases continued to grow. Organizations started to handle more data and required more sophisticated features to manage it. This led to innovations in indexing, query optimization, and transaction management. Indexing allowed for faster data retrieval by creating additional data structures that speeded up search operations. Query optimization techniques improved the efficiency of SQL queries, reducing the amount of time it took to retrieve data from large datasets. Transaction management became more advanced, with features such as ACID (Atomicity, Consistency, Isolation, Durability) properties ensuring that database transactions were reliable and could handle errors or interruptions.

One of the most notable developments during this time was the rise of Object-Relational Database Management Systems (ORDBMS). These systems were designed to bridge the gap between the relational model and object-oriented programming. ORDBMS allowed for more complex data structures, such as multimedia content, to be stored alongside traditional relational data. This opened up new possibilities for managing data in a way that was more aligned with the needs of modern applications. Object-relational databases paved the way for innovations such as spatial databases, which handle geographical data, and XML databases, which handle data in a format suitable for web-based applications.

In the 2000s, the focus of relational database development shifted toward scalability, reliability, and high availability. As the internet and e-commerce exploded, the demand for databases that could handle large volumes of concurrent transactions and provide fast responses grew significantly. Companies needed databases that could scale horizontally across multiple servers and handle the increased load. This led to the rise of distributed databases, which allowed data to be spread across multiple physical locations, improving both availability and performance. The ability to replicate data across multiple servers became a key feature for maintaining uptime and preventing data loss in case of server failures.

The development of cloud computing in the 2010s brought about a new era for relational databases. Cloud services such as Amazon Web Services (AWS), Microsoft Azure, and Google Cloud began to offer managed database services that took care of the infrastructure and scaling needs of businesses. This allowed organizations to focus more on their core business operations and less on database administration. Cloud-based relational databases offered a number of advantages, including automated backups, built-in scalability, and cost-effective pricing models that allowed businesses to pay only for the resources they used. Cloud technologies also led to the development of hybrid databases that combined relational and NoSQL features, enabling organizations to handle both structured and unstructured data.

Today, RDBMS continue to evolve to meet the needs of modern businesses and applications. The demand for real-time data processing, machine learning, and big data analytics has introduced new challenges and opportunities for relational databases. Technologies such as in-memory databases, which store data in the system's memory rather than on disk, have emerged to provide faster data processing. Additionally, relational databases are being integrated with other data management systems, such as NoSQL databases, to provide more flexible and scalable solutions for organizations that handle both structured and unstructured data. While the relational model is still the foundation for many applications, the integration of multiple data management paradigms is becoming more common.

The future of relational database management lies in its continued ability to adapt to changing technological landscapes. As businesses continue to collect and process larger and more complex datasets, relational databases must evolve to provide faster, more efficient, and more flexible solutions. Despite the rise of NoSQL and other database models, relational databases remain a critical component of enterprise data management strategies due to their proven track record of reliability, scalability, and consistency. With advancements in cloud computing, AI, and machine learning, relational databases will likely continue to be a vital part of the data management ecosystem for years to come, ensuring that data remains accessible, secure, and ready for analysis when needed.

Fundamentals of Relational Databases

A relational database is a system for storing, managing, and retrieving data in a structured manner. Its foundation is the relational model, which organizes data into tables that are related to one another based on shared attributes. These tables consist of rows and columns, where each row represents a record, and each column represents a field or attribute of that record. The relational model, developed by Edgar F. Codd in the 1970s, was a breakthrough in how data could be stored and manipulated efficiently, leading to the development of relational database management systems (RDBMS) that have become ubiquitous in modern computing.

The fundamental concept of a relational database is its ability to store data in tables that are logically connected. These connections between tables are made using keys, which are special columns that help to identify records and establish relationships between different sets of data. The most important type of key in a relational database is the primary key, which uniquely identifies each record in a table. Each table in a relational database should have one and only one primary key to ensure that each record can be retrieved without ambiguity. A primary key is typically a field that contains unique values, such as an ID number or a username, making it an essential part of maintaining data integrity and preventing duplicates.

Another key concept in relational databases is the foreign key, which is a field in one table that links to the primary key in another table. Foreign keys establish relationships between tables, allowing data from one table to be associated with data in another table. These relationships are fundamental to the relational model, as they allow users to query data across multiple tables and combine information in meaningful ways. Foreign keys help ensure referential integrity, meaning that relationships between tables are consistent. For instance, a foreign key can prevent a user from inserting data into a table if it references a non-existent record in another table, helping to maintain the accuracy and reliability of the database.

One of the core advantages of relational databases is their ability to organize and manipulate data using a structured query language (SQL). SQL allows users to retrieve, insert, update, and delete data from relational tables using a standardized syntax. It also allows for complex queries that involve multiple tables and sophisticated operations such as joins, aggregations, and sorting. SQL has become the universal language for relational databases, and its power lies in its simplicity and flexibility, allowing users to perform a wide range of tasks, from simple data retrieval to complex analytical queries. Through SQL, users can access the data stored in relational databases and perform operations on it without needing to understand the underlying physical storage mechanisms.

Normalization is another key principle in the design of relational databases. The process of normalization involves organizing data within a database to reduce redundancy and dependency. By following a series of steps, known as normal forms, database designers can ensure that data is stored in an efficient and logical manner. The goal of normalization is to eliminate anomalies that could arise from data duplication or inconsistencies, such as insert, update, and delete anomalies. For instance, if a database table stores the same data in multiple places, it becomes difficult to update that data consistently, leading to errors and inefficiencies. Normalization helps address these issues by breaking down data into smaller, more manageable units that can be linked together using keys.

There are several normal forms, each with its own set of rules for organizing data. The first normal form (1NF) ensures that each column in a table contains only atomic, indivisible values, while the second normal form (2NF) eliminates partial dependency by ensuring that non-key attributes are fully dependent on the primary key. The third normal form (3NF) goes further by eliminating transitive dependency, where non-key attributes depend on other non-key attributes. Higher normal forms, such as Boyce-Codd Normal Form (BCNF) and fourth normal form (4NF), address even more specific types of data redundancy. However, while normalization is important for maintaining data integrity, it can sometimes lead to performance trade-offs, especially when complex queries are needed, as it may require joining multiple tables. In such cases, denormalization, the process of introducing some redundancy back into the database, can be used to improve query performance.

Another fundamental concept in relational databases is data integrity, which refers to the accuracy and consistency of the data stored within the system. Data integrity is maintained through constraints, which are rules applied to the data that help ensure its correctness. Some common types of constraints include primary key constraints, foreign key constraints, and unique constraints. Primary key constraints ensure that each record in a table is unique, while foreign key constraints maintain referential integrity between tables. Unique constraints ensure that no two records in a table have the same value for a specific column or set of columns. These constraints play a vital role in ensuring that the data stored in relational databases is accurate, consistent, and reliable.

Transactions are a critical aspect of relational databases, as they ensure that operations on the data are performed in a reliable and consistent manner. A transaction is a set of operations that are executed as a single unit of work. The properties of a transaction are defined by the ACID model, which stands for Atomicity, Consistency, Isolation, and Durability. Atomicity ensures that all operations within a transaction are completed successfully or not at all, meaning that the database is never left in an inconsistent state. Consistency ensures that a transaction transforms the database from one valid state to another. Isolation ensures that concurrent transactions do not interfere with each other, and durability guarantees that once a transaction is committed, its effects are permanent, even in the event of a system failure. These properties make transactions essential for ensuring the reliability and integrity of relational databases.

Relational databases have become the standard for managing structured data in a wide variety of applications. From small businesses to large enterprises, RDBMS are used to manage everything from customer data to financial records. The versatility and robustness of relational databases, combined with the power of SQL, have made them a cornerstone of modern data management. Although newer database models, such as NoSQL, have gained popularity in recent years, relational databases remain a dominant force in the data management landscape. Their ability to handle large amounts of structured data, enforce data integrity, and provide powerful querying capabilities makes them indispensable in today's data-driven world. The fundamentals of relational databases, including the concepts of tables, keys, normalization, and transactions, continue to form the foundation of database management practices and will likely remain relevant for years to come.

Database Models and Their Role in Design

Database models are fundamental frameworks that define how data is structured, stored, and accessed within a database system. These models provide the foundation for organizing and managing data efficiently, influencing how users interact with the data and how the database itself is built and maintained. Over the years, several database models have emerged, each serving different needs and purposes in various contexts. The relational model, the hierarchical model, the network model, and the object-oriented model are among the most influential and widely used. Each model has its unique characteristics and plays a critical role in the design of databases to meet specific requirements for performance, scalability, and flexibility.

The relational database model, introduced by Edgar F. Codd in 1970, is the most widely used database model today. It organizes data into tables (also known as relations), where each table consists of rows and columns. Each row represents a record, and each column represents an attribute of that record. This model is based on set theory and uses a declarative query language called SQL (Structured Query Language) to allow users to interact with the database. The relational model emphasizes data integrity, flexibility, and the ability to manage complex queries. It is particularly well-suited for applications that require structured data, such as customer information, financial data, and inventory management. The relational model has influenced the design of a large number of database management systems (RDBMS) such as Oracle, MySQL, and Microsoft SQL Server, making it the standard for data storage and retrieval in most enterprise applications.

The hierarchical model is one of the earliest models of database design and organizes data in a tree-like structure. In this model, data is represented in a series of records, where each record has a parent-child relationship with other records. A single root record exists at the top of the hierarchy, and all other records are linked below it in a tree structure. This model is efficient for representing data with a clear, one-to-many relationship, such as organizational structures or file systems. However, it lacks flexibility, as data is tightly bound to its parent-child relationships, making it difficult to restructure the data without significant changes to the database schema. Despite its limitations, the hierarchical model was widely used in early database systems, such as IBM's Information Management System (IMS), due to its simplicity and performance in handling certain types of queries.

The network model, developed as an extension of the hierarchical model, offers more flexibility by allowing records to have multiple parent-child relationships, creating a more complex structure with many-to-many relationships. In the network model, data is represented as a graph, with records as nodes and relationships as edges. This model allows for more complex relationships between data elements, making it suitable for applications such as telecommunications, where data might need to be linked in a more intricate way. While the network model is more flexible than the hierarchical model, it still requires careful management and design to avoid data redundancy and maintain referential integrity. Despite its advantages, the network model became less popular with the rise of the relational model, which offered simpler and more powerful ways to manage complex data relationships.

The object-oriented database model is based on object-oriented programming principles, which combine both data and the methods that operate on the data into a single unit, known as an object. In object-oriented databases, data is organized as objects, similar to how it is handled in object-oriented programming languages like Java or C++. This model allows for more complex data structures, such as multimedia files, spatial data, and other non-traditional data types. Object-oriented databases are particularly useful in applications that require advanced data representations, such as computer-aided design (CAD) systems, scientific research databases, and real-time systems. The object-oriented model supports features like inheritance, polymorphism, and encapsulation, allowing for better representation of real-world entities and their behaviors. However, object-oriented databases are not as widely adopted as relational databases, primarily because of their complexity and the limited availability of supporting tools and resources.

The role of database models in design is to provide a framework that guides how data is organized and how it can be accessed efficiently. When designing a database, the choice of model depends on the specific requirements of the application, the type of data being handled, and the scalability needs of the system. The relational model, for example, is well-suited for applications with structured data and complex queries, while the hierarchical and network models may be more appropriate for applications with simpler, well-defined relationships. The object-oriented model, on the other hand, is ideal for applications that require more sophisticated data representations and complex data interactions.

In the design process, the database model helps define the structure of the data and the relationships between different data elements. This process is essential for ensuring that the database can handle the required operations efficiently while maintaining data integrity and minimizing redundancy. During database design, the choice of model impacts several factors, including data access patterns, query performance, and how easily the system can scale as data volumes grow. For example, relational databases are designed to handle large volumes of structured data and support powerful query languages like SQL, making them ideal for transactional systems. On the other hand, hierarchical and network databases may perform better in systems with simpler relationships but struggle with more complex queries or changes in the database structure.

Additionally, the database model chosen during the design phase also affects how easily the database can evolve over time. In the relational model, normalization techniques are used to ensure that the database schema is well-organized and efficient, but changes to the schema can be more challenging as the database grows. Object-oriented databases, with their more flexible approach to data, may allow for easier changes to the database structure, especially in systems where new data types or relationships are frequently introduced. However, the learning curve for object-oriented databases can be steeper, and the technology is less mature compared to relational databases.

Furthermore, the design of a database is not just about the model itself but also about how the model is implemented and optimized for the specific needs of the application. Factors such as indexing, caching, partitioning, and replication all play a role in ensuring that the database performs well and can handle high volumes of data and transactions. A well-designed database model, combined with efficient database management practices, ensures that the system can scale, remain reliable, and provide fast access to data, which is crucial for meeting the needs of modern applications that rely on large amounts of data.

The choice of database model is a crucial decision that impacts not only the performance and efficiency of the system but also its ability to adapt to changing requirements and data complexities over time. Each database model has its strengths and weaknesses, and the role of the model in database design is to provide a structure that aligns with the application's goals while ensuring that the data is managed in the most effective way possible. Whether using relational, hierarchical, network, or object-oriented models, the database model serves as the foundation upon which the entire database system is built, making it one of the most critical aspects of database design.

Relational Database Design: An Introduction

Relational database design is a critical process in the development of an efficient and effective database system. The design process determines how data will be structured, stored, and accessed within the database, and it directly influences the performance, integrity, and scalability of the system. At the core of relational database design is the goal of creating a schema that represents the real-world entities and relationships while ensuring that the data is stored in a way that minimizes redundancy, maintains consistency, and supports efficient querying. Understanding relational database design is crucial for anyone involved in developing or maintaining databases, as it ensures that the system will meet both current and future needs of the organization.

The foundation of relational database design lies in the principles of the relational model, which organizes data into tables (also called relations). Each table consists of rows and columns, where each row represents a record and each column represents an attribute or field of that record. The relational model enables data to be represented in a simple, structured, and understandable manner, which makes it easy to work with and manipulate using SQL. One of the key goals of relational database design is to determine the appropriate tables, attributes, and relationships that will effectively represent the data for a given application.

One of the first steps in relational database design is identifying the entities that need to be represented. An entity is any object or concept that can have data stored about it. For example, in a university database, entities might include students, courses, and professors. Each of these entities will become a table in the database, and each entity will have a set of attributes that describe it. A student entity might have attributes such as name, student ID, and date of birth, while a course entity might have attributes such as course name, course code, and the professor teaching the course. Defining entities and their attributes is a fundamental part of the design process because it sets the foundation for how the data will be structured.

Once the entities have been identified, the next step is to define the relationships between these entities. Relationships are the connections between different entities that are essential for the proper functioning of the database. For example, a student may enroll in multiple courses, and a course may have multiple students enrolled in it. This is a many-to-many relationship between the student and course entities. Identifying and defining the relationships between entities is crucial, as it allows the database to store data in a way that reflects how the real-world entities interact with each other. Relationships can be classified into three types: one-to-one, one-to-many, and many-to-many. A one-to-one relationship means that each record in one table is related to one and only one record in another table. A one-to-many relationship means that one record in one table is related to multiple records in another table. A many-to-many relationship means that multiple records in one table are related to multiple records in another table. In many-to-many relationships, a junction table is often used to break the relationship into two one-to-many relationships.

Normalization is a key technique used in relational database design to ensure that the database schema is efficient and free from unnecessary redundancy. The process of normalization involves organizing the data into separate tables so that each table represents a single subject and its attributes. By doing so, the database design reduces duplication of data, which helps maintain consistency and integrity. The goal of normalization is to ensure that the database is free from anomalies that could arise during data insertion, deletion, or updating. These anomalies, such as update, delete, and insert anomalies, occur when redundant data causes inconsistencies in the database. Normalization is achieved by applying a series of normal forms, each of which eliminates a specific type of redundancy or dependency.

The first normal form (1NF) requires that each column in a table contain atomic values, meaning that each value must be indivisible. This ensures that the data in the table is organized in a way that allows for efficient querying. The second normal form (2NF) further refines the design by ensuring that all non-key attributes are fully dependent on the primary key of the table. This eliminates partial dependency, where a non-key attribute depends only on part of a composite primary key. The third normal form (3NF) eliminates transitive dependencies, where non-key attributes depend on other non-key attributes. Higher normal forms, such as Boyce-Codd normal form (BCNF) and fourth normal form (4NF), further refine the design to eliminate even more complex types of redundancy and dependency. While normalization is important for maintaining data integrity, it is not always the best solution for every scenario. In some cases, denormalization, or the process of introducing some level of redundancy back into the database, may be used to improve performance, especially when dealing with complex queries or large datasets.

The choice of primary keys is another important aspect of relational database design. A primary key is a field or set of fields that uniquely identifies each record in a table. Primary keys ensure that each record can be accessed without ambiguity and are essential for maintaining data integrity. In addition to primary keys, foreign keys play a crucial role in relational database design. A foreign key is a field in one table that is used to establish a link to the primary key of another table. Foreign keys are used to represent relationships between tables and ensure referential integrity, meaning that the relationships between records in different tables are consistent.

Another important consideration in relational database design is ensuring that the database schema is flexible and scalable. As data grows and evolves over time, the database schema must be able to accommodate changes without requiring significant rework or disruption to the system. This requires careful planning and an understanding of how the data will be used and accessed over time. Designing for scalability involves considering factors such as indexing, query optimization, and partitioning to ensure that the database can handle large volumes of data and high transaction loads. A well-designed relational database can scale to accommodate increasing amounts of data and ensure that performance remains high even as the system grows.

In addition to the structural aspects of design, it is also important to consider the functional requirements of the database. This includes understanding the types of queries that will be run against the database, as well as any constraints or rules that need to be enforced. For example, a database used to track inventory may require constraints to ensure that quantities are always non-negative, while a database used for financial transactions may need to enforce rules to ensure data consistency and prevent fraud. Understanding the functional requirements of the system is crucial for designing a database that meets both the business needs and technical specifications of the application.

Relational database design is an essential part of database development, and the process of designing a relational database requires careful planning, attention to detail, and a deep understanding of both the data and the application it serves. By focusing on creating a well-structured, efficient, and scalable schema, designers can ensure that the database will meet the needs of the organization and provide reliable, accurate, and fast access to data. Proper relational database design not only facilitates the efficient storage and retrieval of data but also supports the long-term success of the system by ensuring that it can adapt to changing requirements and growing data volumes.

Normalization: The Key to Effective Database Design

Normalization is a fundamental process in relational database design that aims to organize the data within a database in a way that reduces redundancy and improves data integrity. The process of normalization involves decomposing a database into multiple tables and ensuring that each table represents a single concept, reducing the likelihood of data anomalies. Through normalization, a database can be designed to handle complex queries, maintain consistency, and ensure that data can be updated, inserted, or deleted without introducing errors or inconsistencies. Understanding the principles and steps of normalization is essential for creating efficient and reliable databases that can scale and adapt to changing requirements over time.

The primary goal of normalization is to eliminate redundancy in a database design. Data redundancy occurs when the same piece of data is stored in multiple places within the database. This redundancy can lead to several issues, such as inconsistencies in the data, difficulty in updating records, and inefficient use of storage. By normalizing the database, data is stored only once, which reduces the potential for errors and makes the database more efficient in terms of storage and performance. In addition to reducing redundancy, normalization also ensures that the data is logically structured, allowing for more efficient querying and easier maintenance.

Normalization is accomplished through a series of steps known as normal forms. These normal forms represent progressively stricter rules for organizing the data. The most common normal forms are the first normal form (1NF), the second normal form (2NF), and the third normal form (3NF), though there are higher normal forms that address even more complex cases of redundancy. Each normal form builds upon the previous one, with the goal of eliminating different types of redundancy and ensuring that the data structure is as efficient and logical as possible.

The first normal form (1NF) is the simplest and the foundational rule of normalization. A table is in 1NF if it contains only atomic, indivisible values in each of its columns. This means that each column must contain a single value and not a set or list of values. For example, a table that stores customer information should not have a column that contains multiple phone numbers for a single customer. Instead, each phone number should be stored in its own record, ensuring that each column contains only one value per row. By enforcing 1NF, we eliminate repeating groups of data and ensure that the database is structured in a way that allows for efficient querying and maintenance.

The second normal form (2NF) builds upon the first normal form by eliminating partial dependency. A table is in 2NF if it is in 1NF and if all non-key attributes are fully dependent on the primary key. In other words, every non-key column in the table must depend on the entire primary key, and not just a part of it. This is particularly important in tables with composite primary keys, which are primary keys made up of more than one column. For example, consider a table that stores information about student enrollments in courses, with a composite primary key made up of the student ID and the course ID. If there are attributes such as the student's name or the professor's name in this table, they are partially dependent on just the student ID or just the course ID. To achieve 2NF, these attributes should be moved to separate tables where they are fully dependent on a single key.

The third normal form (3NF) takes the process of normalization even further by eliminating transitive dependencies. A table is in 3NF if it is in 2NF and if there are no transitive dependencies between non-key attributes. A transitive dependency occurs when a non-key attribute depends on another non-key attribute, rather than depending directly on the primary key. For example, if a table stores information about employees, and one of the columns stores the name of the employee's department, the department's name may be dependent on the department ID, which in turn depends on the employee's ID. This creates a transitive dependency. To achieve 3NF, the department information should be moved to a separate table that is linked to the employee table through the department ID, eliminating the transitive dependency and ensuring that all non-key attributes are directly dependent on the primary key.

Higher normal forms, such as Boyce-Codd normal form (BCNF) and fourth normal form (4NF), address even more specific types of redundancy and dependency. BCNF is a stricter version of 3NF that deals with situations where there are multiple candidate keys in a table and where dependencies between these keys can cause redundancy. Fourth normal form (4NF) deals with multi-valued dependencies, where a single record may have multiple independent sets of data that should be separated into different tables. Although higher normal forms are often less commonly used in practice, they provide additional refinement to ensure that databases are as free from redundancy as possible.

While normalization is crucial for ensuring data integrity and efficiency, it is not without its trade-offs. One of the challenges of normalization is that it can lead to a large number of tables, which may require more complex queries to retrieve data. In particular, when data is spread across many tables, queries often need to join multiple tables to obtain the necessary information. This can result in slower query performance, particularly with large datasets. To mitigate this, some databases may employ techniques such as indexing, caching, and query optimization to speed up data retrieval.

In some cases, denormalization may be used as a strategy to improve performance. Denormalization involves intentionally introducing some level of redundancy into the database in order to reduce the complexity of queries and improve retrieval times. While denormalization can improve performance by reducing the need for complex joins, it also reintroduces the risk of data anomalies and inconsistencies. Therefore, denormalization should be used judiciously and only when the performance benefits outweigh the potential drawbacks.

Normalization also plays a crucial role in ensuring that databases remain consistent as they evolve over time. As new data is added to the system or as requirements change, the structure of the database may need to be modified. A well-normalized database is more flexible and easier to modify because the relationships between data elements are clearly defined. For example, adding a new attribute to a table or changing the way two tables are related is less likely to cause problems if the database is properly normalized. In contrast, a poorly designed database with excessive redundancy is more likely to encounter issues when changes are needed, leading to difficulties in maintaining and evolving the system.

In addition to improving data integrity and performance, normalization also helps with maintaining the overall quality of the database. By ensuring that data is organized logically and consistently, normalization makes it easier to manage and audit the data, which is critical for applications in fields such as finance, healthcare, and research. In these fields, maintaining high-quality data is essential to ensuring the accuracy of reports, making informed decisions, and complying with regulations.

Normalization is a critical aspect of relational database design that helps to ensure that data is stored in a way that minimizes redundancy, maintains consistency, and supports efficient querying. The process of normalization involves applying a series of rules, known as normal forms, to organize the data and eliminate unnecessary dependencies. While normalization can sometimes lead to performance trade-offs, its benefits in terms of data integrity and ease of maintenance make it a key practice in designing effective and reliable relational databases.

Entity-Relationship Modeling in Database Design

Entity-Relationship (ER) modeling is a crucial technique in database design that helps represent the data requirements of an application in a clear and organized manner. It serves as a blueprint for designing a database by visually capturing the entities involved, the relationships between them, and the constraints that govern the data. The ER model, introduced by Peter Chen in 1976, provides a way to conceptualize the data structure before it is implemented in a physical database system. This method allows database designers to create an efficient and effective design that aligns with the needs of the business or application.

At the core of ER modeling is the concept of an entity, which represents a real-world object or concept that can have data stored about it. An entity could be anything relevant to the domain of the system, such as a customer, a product, a course, or an employee. Each entity is characterized by a set of attributes, which are the data elements that describe the entity. For example, an employee entity might have attributes such as employee ID, name, address, and hire date. Identifying the entities that are relevant to the system is one of the first steps in ER modeling, as it helps determine the structure of the database and ensures that all necessary data will be captured.

Once the entities are identified, the next step in the ER modeling process is to define the relationships between them. Relationships describe how entities are associated with one another in the context of the system. For example, a customer might place an order, or an employee might manage a department. These relationships are essential for understanding how the data will be linked across different entities. Relationships can vary in complexity and can be classified into three types: one-to-one, one-to-many, and many-to-many. A one-to-one relationship means that a single record in one entity is associated with a single record in another entity. A one-to-many relationship, on the other hand, occurs when a single record in one entity is related to multiple records in another entity. A many-to-many relationship happens when multiple records in one entity are related to multiple records in another entity. Understanding and defining these relationships is critical for ensuring that the database schema will accurately represent how the data interacts within the system.

In addition to defining entities and relationships, ER modeling also involves establishing constraints, which are rules that govern the data within the system. Constraints are used to ensure that the data remains consistent, valid, and accurate. For example, an integrity constraint might specify that a customer's email address must be unique, or that a product's price cannot be negative. These constraints are essential for maintaining data quality and ensuring that the system operates as expected. One important type of constraint in ER modeling is the cardinality constraint, which defines the number of occurrences of one entity that can be associated with the occurrences of another entity. For instance, a cardinality constraint might state that a department can have many employees, but each employee can only belong to one department. Defining these constraints upfront is an essential part of the ER modeling process because it ensures that the final database design will enforce the necessary rules and behaviors for the data.

Another important concept in ER modeling is the idea of identifying primary keys and foreign keys. A primary key is a unique identifier for each record in an entity, ensuring that each instance of the entity can be uniquely identified. For example, in an employee table, the employee ID might serve as the primary key, uniquely identifying each employee record. A foreign key, on the other hand, is an attribute in one entity that links to the primary key of another entity, establishing a relationship between the two. For instance, an order table might have a foreign key that links to the customer table, indicating which customer placed the order. The use of primary and foreign keys is vital for maintaining referential integrity in the database, ensuring that the relationships between entities are consistent and that no orphaned records are created.

As ER modeling is a conceptual design tool, it is often used in the early stages of database design to lay the groundwork for the physical implementation of the database. The ER diagram, a visual representation of the ER model, is typically used to illustrate the entities, attributes, and relationships in the system. This diagram serves as a useful tool for communicating the design to stakeholders, developers, and database administrators. It provides a high-level view of the system that can be easily understood by non-technical users, which is crucial for ensuring that the database design meets the needs of the business.

Once the ER model is complete, it can be translated into a relational schema, which is the blueprint for creating the actual tables and relationships in a relational database management system (RDBMS). During this process, the entities become tables, the attributes become columns, and the relationships between entities are implemented through foreign keys. The ER model also helps identify potential issues with data redundancy, integrity, and performance that may arise during the physical design phase. For example, if a many-to-many relationship is detected between two entities, it may be necessary to introduce a junction table to properly represent the relationship in the database.

ER modeling is not only useful for the initial design of a database, but it also plays a critical role in database maintenance and evolution. As business needs and data requirements change over time, the database schema may need to be modified to accommodate new data or features. An ER model can serve as a reference point for understanding how the data is structured, making it easier to identify where changes need to be made. Whether adding new entities, modifying relationships, or introducing new constraints, the ER model provides a clear map of the data structure that helps guide these changes.

The process of ER modeling is also invaluable when dealing with complex databases that involve many entities and relationships. In such cases, ER diagrams help to break down the system into manageable components, making it easier to understand the overall structure of the data and how the various elements interact. This clarity is especially important in large-scale applications, such as enterprise resource planning (ERP) systems or customer relationship management (CRM) software, where the database design must support a wide range of business processes and functions.

In summary, entity-relationship modeling is an essential technique for database design that provides a structured, systematic approach to representing the data and its relationships within a system. By defining entities, relationships, and constraints, ER modeling helps ensure that the database will be logically organized, efficient, and able to handle the needs of the application. Whether used in the early stages of design, as a tool for communication, or as a reference for future database modifications, ER modeling serves as a foundational element of effective database development.

Constraints in Relational Databases: Types and Importance

Constraints in relational databases play a critical role in maintaining the integrity, consistency, and reliability of the data stored within the system. They are rules or restrictions applied to the data in the database to ensure that the data remains accurate, meaningful, and free from anomalies. Without constraints, a database could allow incorrect or inconsistent data to be inserted, leading to unreliable information and errors in processing. Constraints are integral to enforcing the rules that govern data relationships, ensuring data validity, and preventing issues such as duplication, missing values, and data integrity violations. These constraints are essential in every stage of the database lifecycle, from design to maintenance, and they help ensure that the database functions as intended.

The most common types of constraints in relational databases include primary key constraints, foreign key constraints, unique constraints, check constraints, and not null constraints. Each of these constraints serves a distinct purpose, contributing to the overall integrity and reliability of the database. Primary key constraints, for example, are used to ensure that each record in a table is unique and identifiable. A primary key is a field or set of fields in a table that uniquely identifies each record. It is crucial for the proper functioning of the database, as it allows other tables to reference records in a way that ensures data consistency. The primary key guarantees that no two rows in a table can have the same value for the primary key column(s), preventing duplication and maintaining the uniqueness of each record.

Foreign key constraints are equally important, as they help maintain the relationships between different tables in the database. A foreign key is a column in one table that references the primary key of another table. This relationship ensures that the data in one table is consistent with the data in another table. For example, in an order management system, a foreign key in the order table might reference the customer table's primary key, establishing a relationship between the orders and the customers who placed them. Foreign key constraints prevent orphaned records from appearing in the database, ensuring that every record in a child table has a corresponding record in the parent table. This is crucial for maintaining referential integrity, which ensures that relationships between data entities are valid and consistent.

Unique constraints are another form of data integrity enforcement in relational databases. These constraints ensure that no two rows in a table can have the same value for a specific column or set of columns. While the primary key ensures uniqueness across the entire table, the unique constraint allows for additional columns to be defined with the same level of uniqueness. For instance, in a table of employees, a unique constraint might be applied to the email address column to ensure that no two employees share the same email address. This constraint prevents duplicate values from being entered into a column and helps maintain the accuracy of the data stored in the table.

Check constraints are used to ensure that the values in a column satisfy a specific condition or set of conditions. These constraints are useful for enforcing business rules and ensuring that data falls within acceptable ranges or categories. For example, a check constraint could be applied to a salary column to ensure that salaries are always greater than zero. Similarly, a check constraint could be used in a date column to ensure that the values entered fall within a specific time period. Check constraints help improve the quality of data by preventing invalid or incorrect values from being inserted into the database.

Not null constraints are designed to prevent null values from being inserted into a column. A null value in a relational database represents the absence of a value or an unknown value, and it can sometimes cause issues with data integrity and query results. By applying a not null constraint, a designer ensures that a column must always have a value. This is particularly important in cases where certain attributes are critical to the functioning of the system. For instance, in a customer table, the customer ID column might be defined with a not null constraint because every customer must have a unique identifier. The not null constraint ensures that important data is always provided, preventing incomplete or missing information from being recorded.

The importance of constraints in relational databases cannot be overstated. They are essential for maintaining data quality, preventing errors, and ensuring that the database functions as intended. One of the key reasons constraints are important is that they help prevent data anomalies, such as duplicate records, invalid entries, or orphaned records. For example, without a primary key constraint, it would be possible to insert two records with identical values, causing confusion and inconsistency in the data. Without foreign key constraints, relationships between tables could be violated, leading to referential integrity issues where records in one table no longer correspond to records in another. These types of issues can have serious consequences, especially in systems where accurate data is critical, such as financial or healthcare applications.

Constraints also play a vital role in improving the performance and efficiency of the database. By enforcing rules on the data at the time of insertion, update, or deletion, constraints reduce the need for manual validation or post-processing of data. This can lead to faster and more efficient operations, as the database engine can automatically enforce the rules without requiring additional logic from the application. Additionally, constraints such as unique indexes and foreign keys can improve query performance by optimizing the database's ability to retrieve related data. For example, indexing a column with a unique constraint can speed up lookups and searches, as the database can quickly determine whether a value already exists in the table.

Another important aspect of constraints is their role in ensuring data consistency across different systems and applications. In modern applications, data is often distributed across multiple systems or databases, and ensuring consistency between these systems is critical. Constraints provide a way to enforce rules at the database level, reducing the likelihood of errors or inconsistencies when data is exchanged between systems. For instance, when a record is inserted into one database, foreign key constraints can ensure that related records in other databases or tables remain consistent, preventing the creation of inconsistent or incomplete data relationships.

Furthermore, constraints are crucial for maintaining compliance with regulatory requirements and industry standards. In many sectors, such as finance, healthcare, and e-commerce, there are strict regulations governing the storage and handling of data. Constraints help enforce these regulations by ensuring that the data meets specific rules and standards. For example, in a healthcare database, constraints might be used to ensure that patient records are properly linked to the correct provider and that sensitive data is stored securely. Similarly, in financial applications, constraints might ensure that transactions are always balanced and that accounts do not go into negative balances.

While constraints are essential for ensuring data integrity, there are also considerations to keep in mind when designing and implementing them. For instance, while foreign key constraints help enforce referential integrity, they can also introduce performance overhead, especially in large-scale databases with millions of records. In some cases, careful planning and optimization may be necessary to balance the need for data integrity with the system's performance requirements. Additionally, constraints can sometimes conflict with business logic or cause issues with data migration or integration. Therefore, it is important for database designers and administrators to carefully consider the types of constraints to apply, as well as their impact on system performance and usability.

In conclusion, constraints are an essential component of relational databases that help ensure data integrity, consistency, and reliability. Through the use of primary keys, foreign keys, unique constraints, check constraints, and not null constraints, databases can maintain high-quality data, prevent anomalies, and support efficient query processing. Constraints also play a crucial role in ensuring that data is compliant with regulatory requirements and industry standards. By enforcing rules at the database level, constraints reduce the risk of data errors and inconsistencies, leading to more reliable and accurate database systems. The importance of constraints in relational databases cannot be understated, as they form the foundation of a well-designed and functional database.

Data Integrity and Validation in Relational Databases

Data integrity and validation are essential components of relational databases that ensure the accuracy, consistency, and reliability of the data stored within a system. In any database, maintaining data integrity is crucial for ensuring that the data is trustworthy and meets the required standards. Data validation, on the other hand, involves ensuring that the data entered into the database adheres to predefined rules or constraints. These two concepts work together to prevent errors, inconsistencies, and redundancies in the database, which can ultimately lead to faulty data analysis, incorrect decision-making, and a loss of confidence in the system. In relational databases, where complex relationships between data entities are common, enforcing data integrity and validation becomes even more vital.

Data integrity refers to the accuracy and consistency of data across the database. In relational databases, the integrity of data is maintained through various constraints that are defined during the design phase. These constraints help ensure that the data stored in the database is valid, meaningful, and consistent with the rules of the system. There are several types of integrity constraints in relational databases, including entity integrity, referential integrity, and domain integrity. Each type of integrity plays a specific role in ensuring the quality of the data stored in the system.

Entity integrity is one of the fundamental principles of data integrity in relational databases. It ensures that each record in a table can be uniquely identified. This is typically achieved by defining a primary key for each table. The primary key is a field or set of fields that uniquely identifies a record within a table. For example, in a customer table, the customer ID might serve as the primary key. Entity integrity ensures that no two records in the table can have the same primary key value, preventing duplicate entries and ensuring that each record can be retrieved or updated reliably. Without entity integrity, it would be difficult to manage records, leading to potential errors in querying and reporting.

Referential integrity is another critical aspect of data integrity. It ensures that relationships between tables are consistent and valid. In relational databases, tables are often related to one another using foreign keys. A foreign key is a column in one table that links to the primary key of another table. For example, in an order management system, an order table might contain a foreign key that references the customer table's primary key, establishing a relationship between orders and customers. Referential integrity ensures that the data in the foreign key column always corresponds to an existing record in the referenced table. This prevents the creation of orphaned records, where a foreign key in one table points to a record that no longer exists in the referenced table. By enforcing referential integrity, relational databases ensure that relationships between data entities are maintained correctly and that no data is lost or becomes inconsistent.

Domain integrity ensures that the data stored in each column of a table conforms to the expected type, format, and range. Each column in a table has a defined data type, such as integer, varchar, or date, which specifies the kind of data that can be stored in that column. Domain integrity ensures that only valid values are inserted into the table, and it is often enforced through constraints such as check constraints. For example, a check constraint might be applied to a salary column to ensure that only positive numbers are allowed, or a date column might be constrained to accept only valid dates. By enforcing domain integrity, the database ensures that the data stored is both accurate and meaningful, reducing the likelihood of invalid or inconsistent entries.

In addition to maintaining data integrity, data validation is another essential process in relational databases. Data validation involves ensuring that the data entered into the database adheres to specific rules or business logic defined by the application or system requirements. Validation helps prevent the entry of incorrect or incomplete data that could undermine the integrity of the database. Validation rules can be applied to individual fields, groups of fields, or entire records, depending on the nature of the data and the requirements of the system.

One of the most common forms of data validation is the use of constraints. Constraints are rules applied to the columns in a table to ensure that the data meets certain criteria. For example, a not-null constraint can be applied to a column to ensure that every record in the table has a value for that column. A unique constraint ensures that no two records in the table have the same value for a specified column, while a check constraint can be used to enforce specific rules for the data, such as ensuring that a value falls within a certain range or that it matches a specific pattern. These constraints help to validate the data as it is inserted, updated, or deleted from the database, ensuring that only valid data is allowed into the system.

Data validation can also be enforced through triggers and stored procedures. A trigger is a database object that is automatically executed or fired when a specific event, such as an insert, update, or delete operation, occurs on a table. Triggers can be used to perform complex validation logic before or after data changes, ensuring that the data meets specific criteria. For example, a trigger might be used to check that a user's account balance is not negative before processing a transaction. Stored procedures, on the other hand, are precompiled SQL statements that can be executed to perform validation or other operations. Stored procedures can be used to validate data in a more complex way, such as performing calculations or checking business rules that span multiple tables.

In addition to constraints, triggers, and stored procedures, data validation can also be handled at the application level. In many cases, the user interface or the application logic is responsible for performing initial checks on the data before it is sent to the database. For example, when a user enters a form with personal information, the application might validate that the email address follows a correct format, that required fields are not empty, or that the password meets the necessary security criteria. This initial validation helps catch common data entry errors before they reach the database, preventing invalid or incomplete data from being submitted.

The importance of data integrity and validation in relational databases extends beyond ensuring the accuracy of individual records. These processes also contribute to the overall reliability and functionality of the database. When data is validated and consistent, it becomes easier to generate accurate reports, perform data analysis, and make informed decisions based on the information stored in the database. Data integrity and validation also help maintain the reputation of the organization or system by ensuring that data is accurate, consistent, and reliable, which is particularly critical in industries such as finance, healthcare, and e-commerce, where errors in data can lead to severe consequences.

Moreover, maintaining data integrity and validation can also help improve the performance of the database. By enforcing rules at the database level, the system can minimize the need for complex error-handling procedures or post-processing to correct invalid data. This leads to more efficient data processing, faster queries, and reduced overhead in maintaining the database. It also reduces the likelihood of data corruption, which can be difficult and costly to fix.

Data integrity and validation are fundamental to the design and operation of relational databases. They ensure that the data stored in the system is accurate, consistent, and meaningful, supporting the reliability and performance of the database. Through the use of constraints, triggers, stored procedures, and application-level validation, relational databases can ensure that only valid and accurate data is allowed into the system, preventing errors and maintaining the integrity of the database. These practices not only improve the quality of the data but also contribute to the overall efficiency and effectiveness of the database system.

Introduction to SQL: The Language of Relational Databases

Structured Query Language, commonly known as SQL, is the standard language used for managing and manipulating data in relational database management systems (RDBMS). It serves as the interface between the user or application and the database, allowing for the creation, modification, querying, and management of data. SQL plays a critical role in database operations, providing a set of tools and commands that enable users to interact with the underlying relational database efficiently. Understanding SQL is essential for anyone working with relational databases, as it is the primary means through which data is stored, retrieved, and modified.

SQL was developed in the 1970s by IBM as part of the development of their relational database system. It was designed to allow users to communicate with databases using a standardized, easy-to-learn language. SQL is based on set theory and relational algebra, which form the mathematical foundation of relational databases. This allows SQL to handle complex queries, relationships, and data operations in a highly efficient manner. Over the years, SQL has become the industry standard for database management, with most modern RDBMS such as MySQL, PostgreSQL, Microsoft SQL Server, and Oracle using SQL as their primary language.

At the core of SQL is the concept of tables, which store the data in a relational database. A table consists of rows and columns, where each row represents a record, and each column represents an attribute of that record. SQL allows users to interact with these tables in various ways, such as inserting new data, updating existing data, and deleting data. SQL commands are categorized into several types, with the most commonly used being Data Definition Language (DDL), Data Manipulation Language (DML), and Data Control Language (DCL). These categories help organize the various types of operations that SQL can perform on a database.

The Data Definition Language (DDL) is used to define and manage the structure of the database. It includes commands such as CREATE, ALTER, and DROP, which allow users to create, modify, or delete tables, schemas, indexes, and other database objects. For example, the CREATE TABLE command is used to create a new table in the database, specifying the columns and their data types. The ALTER TABLE command allows for modifications to the structure of an existing table, such as adding or removing columns. The DROP command is used to delete tables or other database objects entirely. DDL commands are essential for setting up and maintaining the database schema, ensuring that the structure of the database aligns with the needs of the application or business.

Data Manipulation Language (DML) consists of SQL commands that are used to manipulate the data stored within the tables. The most commonly used DML commands are SELECT, INSERT, UPDATE, and DELETE. The SELECT command is used to query the database and retrieve data from one or more tables. It allows users to specify which columns to retrieve, apply filters, sort the results, and even perform calculations on the data. The INSERT command is used to add new records to a table, specifying values for each column. The UPDATE command allows users to modify existing data in a table, either by updating specific columns or by applying changes to all records that match a given condition. The DELETE command is used to remove records from a table, based on specified criteria. DML commands are fundamental to interacting with the data in a relational database, enabling users to add, retrieve, modify, and delete information.

Data Control Language (DCL) commands are used to manage access control and permissions within the database. The most commonly used DCL commands are GRANT and REVOKE. GRANT is used to provide specific permissions to users or roles, such as the ability to SELECT, INSERT, UPDATE, or DELETE data from a table. The REVOKE command removes these permissions from users or roles, effectively restricting their access to certain database operations. DCL commands help ensure that the database is secure and that users only have access to the data and operations they are authorized to use.

One of the key features of SQL is its ability to handle complex queries that involve multiple tables. Relational databases often store data in different tables, with relationships between the tables established through the use of keys. SQL provides powerful tools for joining tables, allowing users to combine data from different sources into a single result set. The most common type of join is the INNER JOIN, which returns only the rows where there is a match between the tables being joined. Other types of joins include LEFT JOIN, RIGHT JOIN, and FULL OUTER JOIN, which return data based on different matching criteria. SQL also supports subqueries, which allow for more advanced querying by nesting one query inside another. This flexibility enables SQL to handle complex data retrieval tasks and support a wide variety of reporting and analysis requirements.

In addition to querying and modifying data, SQL provides a variety of functions and operators that can be used to perform calculations and manipulate data. SQL functions such as COUNT, SUM, AVG, MIN, and MAX are used to perform aggregate calculations on data, such as counting the number of records, calculating the total sum of a column, or finding the minimum or maximum value in a dataset. SQL also includes string functions, date functions, and mathematical functions that allow users to manipulate and transform data. For example, the CONCAT function can be used to combine two or more strings into a single value, while the NOW function can retrieve the current date and time. These functions are invaluable for performing complex data analysis and reporting tasks.

SQL is also highly versatile and adaptable, allowing users to work with different types of data and systems. For example, SQL can be used to work with structured data stored in relational databases, but it is also capable of handling semi-structured and unstructured data in newer database systems such as NoSQL databases. Some variations of SQL, such as PL/SQL (Procedural Language/SQL) in Oracle or T-SQL (Transact-SQL) in Microsoft SQL Server, add procedural features like loops, conditionals, and error handling, allowing users to write more complex scripts and stored procedures. These extensions to SQL enhance its capabilities and make it a powerful tool for database programming and automation.

The power of SQL lies in its ability to interact with large volumes of data efficiently and flexibly. As businesses and organizations increasingly rely on data to make informed decisions, SQL remains the go-to language for managing relational data. It is used by database administrators, developers, analysts, and data scientists to create, maintain, and query databases. SQL's simplicity, combined with its ability to handle complex queries and large datasets, makes it an indispensable tool in modern data management and analysis.

SQL's wide adoption and standardization across different database platforms make it an essential skill for anyone working with relational databases. Its versatility, ease of use, and powerful querying capabilities ensure that it will continue to be the language of choice for managing and manipulating relational data for years to come.

Querying Relational Databases with SQL

Querying relational databases with SQL is an essential skill for anyone working with relational database management systems (RDBMS). SQL

(Structured Query Language) provides a standardized method for interacting with relational databases, allowing users to retrieve, manipulate, and analyze data efficiently. The ability to write effective SQL queries is crucial for obtaining valuable insights from a database, supporting decision-making, and ensuring that data is accurately retrieved and presented. Understanding the fundamental principles of querying and how SQL operates within the context of relational databases is vital for leveraging its full potential.

In relational databases, data is stored in tables, each consisting of rows and columns. Each row represents a record, and each column represents a specific attribute of that record. When querying a relational database, the primary goal is to retrieve specific data that meets certain conditions. SQL provides a powerful set of tools for filtering, sorting, and manipulating data, allowing users to extract the exact information they need. The most basic SQL command for querying data is the SELECT statement. The SELECT statement is used to retrieve data from one or more tables, specifying the columns to return and any criteria for filtering or sorting the results.

A simple SELECT query might look like this: SELECT column1, column2 FROM table_name; This query retrieves data from the specified columns in the given table. However, in most cases, users will need to apply conditions to narrow down the results. The WHERE clause is used to filter the data based on specific criteria. For example, if a user wants to retrieve all records from a customer table where the customer's country is "USA," the query would look like this: SELECT * FROM customers WHERE country = 'USA'; The asterisk (*) is a wildcard that means "all columns," and the WHERE clause filters the records to only those that match the specified condition.

The WHERE clause can use various comparison operators such as equals (=), greater than (>), less than (<), and not equal to (!=), among others. SQL also supports logical operators such as AND, OR, and NOT, which can be combined to create more complex conditions. For instance, to retrieve customers who live in either the USA or Canada, the query would look like this: SELECT * FROM customers WHERE country = 'USA' OR country = 'Canada'; Additionally, SQL allows the use of pattern matching with the LIKE operator, which enables partial matching of string values. For example, to find customers whose names start with "J," the query could be: SELECT * FROM customers WHERE name LIKE 'J%'; The percentage sign (%) is a wildcard that represents any sequence of characters.

In addition to filtering data, SQL allows users to sort the results of a query using the ORDER BY clause. By default, the ORDER BY clause sorts the data in ascending order, but it can also be used to sort the results in descending order by adding the DESC keyword. For example, to retrieve a list of customers sorted by their age in descending order, the query would be: SELECT * FROM customers ORDER BY age DESC; Sorting data is particularly useful when dealing with large datasets, as it allows users to organize the information in a meaningful way and make it easier to analyze.

SQL also provides the ability to aggregate data using functions such as COUNT, SUM, AVG, MIN, and MAX. These functions allow users to perform calculations on data and obtain summarized information. For example, the COUNT function can be used to find the total number of records in a table, while the SUM function can be used to calculate the total value of a numeric column. To find the total sales for a particular product, the query might look like this: SELECT SUM(sales) FROM products WHERE product_name = 'Laptop'; Similarly, the AVG function calculates the average value of a column, and the MIN and MAX functions return the minimum and maximum values, respectively.

Another powerful feature of SQL is its ability to combine data from multiple tables using joins. In relational databases, data is often spread across multiple tables, and the relationships between these tables are established using keys. Joins allow users to combine data from two or more tables based on a related column. The most common type of join is the INNER JOIN, which returns only the rows where there is a match between the tables. For example, to retrieve a list of orders along with the customer information for each order, the query might look like this: SELECT orders.order_id, customers.name FROM orders INNER JOIN customers ON orders.customer_id = customers.customer_id; This query retrieves data from the orders table and the customers table, matching the customer_id column in both tables.

SQL also supports other types of joins, including LEFT JOIN, RIGHT JOIN, and FULL OUTER JOIN, which are used to return different sets of data based on the matching conditions. A LEFT JOIN, for instance, returns all the rows from the left table (the first table) and the matching rows from the right table (the second table), filling in NULL values for the columns of the right table where there is no match. A RIGHT JOIN works in the opposite way, returning all rows from the right table and the matching rows from the left table. A FULL OUTER JOIN returns all rows from both tables, with NULL values for the columns of the table that does not have a matching row.

Subqueries are another powerful feature of SQL, allowing users to nest one query inside another. Subqueries are useful when the result of one query is needed as input for another query. For example, to retrieve the names of customers who have placed orders for a specific product, the query might look like this: SELECT name FROM customers WHERE customer_id IN (SELECT customer_id FROM orders WHERE product_name = 'Laptop'); The subquery retrieves the customer IDs of customers who have placed orders for the specified product, and the outer query uses those IDs to retrieve the corresponding customer names.

SQL also provides the ability to modify data in a table using the INSERT, UPDATE, and DELETE commands. The INSERT statement is used to add new records to a table, specifying the values for each column. For example, to add a new customer to the customers table, the query might be: INSERT INTO customers (name, email, country) VALUES ('John Doe', 'john.doe@example.com', 'USA'); The UPDATE statement is used to modify existing data, allowing users to change the values in one or more columns. For example, to update a customer's email address, the query would look like this: UPDATE customers SET email = 'ncw.cmail@example.com' WHERE customer_id = 1; The DELETE statement is used to remove records from a table based on a specified condition. For example, to delete a customer from the customers table, the query might be: DELETE FROM customers WHERE customer_id = 1;

SQL queries can also be used to create and modify the structure of tables using Data Definition Language (DDL) commands. The CREATE TABLE command is used to create a new table, specifying the columns and their data types. For example, the query to create a table for customers might be: CREATE TABLE customers (customer_id INT PRIMARY KEY, name VARCHAR(100), email VARCHAR(100), country VARCHAR(50)); The ALTER TABLE command allows users to modify the structure of an existing table, such as adding or removing columns. The DROP TABLE command is used to delete an entire table from the database.

The ability to query relational databases effectively with SQL is essential for anyone working with data stored in relational systems. SQL provides a powerful set of tools for retrieving, manipulating, and analyzing data, allowing users to answer complex questions, generate reports, and make data-driven decisions. By mastering SQL, users can interact with relational databases in an efficient and meaningful way, ensuring that the data is used effectively and accurately.

Advanced SQL Queries and Functions

SQL is a powerful language that allows users to interact with relational databases by performing a variety of operations, from simple data retrieval to complex data manipulation and aggregation. As users become more proficient in SQL, they encounter the need for more advanced queries and functions that can handle complex scenarios, large datasets, and sophisticated business logic. Advanced SQL queries and functions provide powerful tools to filter, transform, and aggregate data in ways that go beyond basic operations. These advanced techniques are invaluable for data analysts, developers, and anyone working with large volumes of data, as they help to extract meaningful insights and make data-driven decisions.

One of the foundational concepts in advanced SQL queries is the use of subqueries, also known as nested queries. A subquery is a query that is embedded within another query and is typically used to retrieve a single value or a set of values that will be used in the outer query. Subqueries can be placed in various parts of a SQL statement, such as the SELECT, WHERE, or FROM clauses. A common use of subqueries is in the WHERE clause, where they help filter results based on data from another query. For example, a subquery can be used to retrieve the highest sales value from a sales table and then use that value to filter rows in a products table. This allows for highly dynamic queries that can be adapted to changing data conditions. Subqueries can also be used to return multiple rows or columns, which can then be processed by the outer query.

Another powerful technique in advanced SQL is the use of joins, particularly complex joins that combine data from multiple tables based on relationships between them. While basic joins, such as INNER JOIN, combine rows based on matching values in specified columns, more advanced join types can be used to handle various complex scenarios. For instance, LEFT JOIN returns all rows from the left table and the matching rows from the right table, but if there is no match, NULL values are returned for columns of the right table. RIGHT JOIN operates similarly but returns all rows from the right table and matching rows from the left. FULL OUTER JOIN returns all rows from both tables, with NULL values where there is no match. These advanced join types are particularly useful when dealing with incomplete data or when attempting to identify missing values between related tables. Furthermore, CROSS JOIN, which produces the Cartesian product of two tables, can be used for scenarios where every combination of rows from both tables is required.

Window functions, also known as analytic functions, are another advanced feature of SQL that allows for more complex analysis and reporting. Window functions operate over a specific range of rows, referred to as a "window," which is defined by the user. These functions are useful for performing calculations across sets of rows related to the current row. Window functions can be applied to retrieve running totals, moving averages, ranks, and other complex aggregates that would be difficult to achieve with standard GROUP BY operations. One of the most common window functions is ROW_NUMBER(), which assigns a unique sequential integer to each row within a partition of the result set. This is often used for tasks such as ranking or numbering rows based on a specific criterion. Other popular window functions include RANK(), DENSE_RANK(), and NTILE(), which allow users to perform sophisticated ranking and distribution operations.

CTEs, or Common Table Expressions, are another advanced SQL feature that makes complex queries more readable and manageable. A

CTE is essentially a temporary result set that can be referred to within the execution scope of a SELECT, INSERT, UPDATE, or DELETE statement. CTEs are defined using the WITH keyword and are especially useful for breaking down complex queries into smaller, more manageable parts. This can improve the clarity of SQL code and make it easier to understand and maintain. CTEs are commonly used in recursive queries, which allow for the processing of hierarchical data, such as organizational charts or directory structures. By using a recursive CTE, users can query data that has a parent-child relationship, where each row can be linked to a preceding or succeeding row. Recursive CTEs are particularly valuable for tasks such as calculating totals for all descendants in a hierarchical structure.

Advanced SQL also includes the use of aggregate functions to perform complex data aggregation and analysis. While basic aggregate functions such as SUM, COUNT, AVG, MIN, and MAX are essential for summarizing data, advanced aggregate functions offer additional capabilities. For example, GROUP_CONCAT() allows users to concatenate values from multiple rows into a single string, which can be useful for generating comma-separated lists of related data. Similarly, the HAVING clause can be used in conjunction with aggregate functions to filter results based on aggregated values. This is especially useful when performing group-level filtering after data has been aggregated, such as when you want to filter groups that meet certain conditions based on the calculated totals.

Another advanced SQL concept is the use of conditional logic within queries. SQL provides various methods for implementing conditional logic, allowing users to build queries that adapt to different conditions. The CASE statement is one of the most common ways to introduce conditional logic in SQL queries. It works like an IF-ELSE statement in programming languages, enabling users to specify different outcomes based on certain conditions. For example, the CASE statement can be used to classify data into categories, such as converting a numeric value into a grade or score. This type of conditional logic can be applied in the SELECT, WHERE, and ORDER BY clauses, providing great flexibility in data transformation and analysis. Another useful feature for conditional logic is the COALESCE function, which returns the first non-null value from a list of expressions. This function is often used to handle NULL values and replace them with default values in query results.

The use of indexes is another important aspect of advanced SQL that can significantly improve query performance. Indexes are special data structures that provide quick access to rows in a table based on the values of one or more columns. By creating indexes on frequently queried columns, database administrators can speed up the retrieval of data, especially for large datasets. However, while indexes can improve query performance, they also come with overhead in terms of storage and maintenance, especially when data is inserted, updated, or deleted. Therefore, it is crucial to design and manage indexes carefully to ensure that they provide the desired performance improvements without incurring unnecessary costs.

SQL also supports complex data types and operations that go beyond simple numerical and string data. Many modern relational databases allow users to work with JSON, XML, and spatial data types, which are used to store semi-structured or unstructured data. SQL functions for handling JSON data, such as JSON_EXTRACT() or JSON_AGG(), allow users to query and manipulate JSON objects and arrays directly within the database. Similarly, SQL extensions for spatial data enable users to perform operations on geographic and geometric data types, such as finding the distance between two points or determining if a point lies within a polygon.

Advanced SQL queries and functions provide powerful tools for manipulating, analyzing, and optimizing data within relational databases. As databases grow in size and complexity, these advanced techniques become increasingly necessary for efficiently handling complex datasets and business logic. By mastering advanced SQL concepts such as subqueries, joins, window functions, CTEs, aggregate functions, and conditional logic, users can leverage the full power of relational databases to extract meaningful insights, streamline operations, and solve complex problems. These advanced SQL capabilities are essential for anyone who works with data on a regular basis and wishes to unlock the full potential of their relational database systems.

Transaction Management in Relational Databases

Transaction management in relational databases is a critical aspect of ensuring data consistency, reliability, and integrity. A transaction in a relational database is a logical unit of work that consists of a sequence of operations performed as a single, indivisible unit. These operations typically involve retrieving, inserting, updating, or deleting data in the database. The main goal of transaction management is to ensure that all operations within a transaction are executed successfully, or if any part of the transaction fails, the entire transaction is rolled back, leaving the database in a consistent state. Transaction management helps maintain the integrity of the database, even in the event of errors, system crashes, or power failures.

The concept of transactions is built upon the ACID properties, which stand for Atomicity, Consistency, Isolation, and Durability. These properties define the behavior and guarantees of transactions in relational databases. The first property, atomicity, ensures that a transaction is treated as a single unit of work. This means that all operations within a transaction must either complete successfully or be entirely undone if any part of the transaction fails. If an error occurs during the transaction, the database is reverted to its state before the transaction began, ensuring that no partial changes are made to the data. Atomicity guarantees that the database will not be left in an inconsistent or partially updated state.

The second property, consistency, ensures that a transaction takes the database from one valid state to another valid state. Before a transaction begins, the database must be in a consistent state, and once the transaction is complete, the database must also be in a consistent state. This means that all integrity constraints, such as foreign keys, primary keys, and other business rules, must be maintained during the transaction. If a transaction violates any of these constraints, it will be rolled back to preserve the consistency of the database. The consistency property guarantees that the data remains accurate and reliable, even as it is being modified by multiple transactions.

Isolation is the third ACID property, and it refers to the degree to which the operations of one transaction are isolated from the operations of other transactions. In a multi-user database environment, transactions are often executed concurrently, and isolation ensures that the operations of one transaction do not interfere with the operations of another. Isolation prevents issues such as dirty reads, non-repeatable reads, and phantom reads, which can occur when one transaction reads data that is being modified by another transaction. To achieve isolation, relational databases use different isolation levels, which determine the extent to which transactions are allowed to interact with each other. These isolation levels include READ UNCOMMITTED, READ COMMITTED, REPEATABLE READ, and SERIALIZABLE, with each level providing a different level of isolation between transactions.

The final ACID property, durability, ensures that once a transaction has been committed, its effects are permanent and cannot be undone, even in the event of a system crash or power failure. Once a transaction is completed and committed, the changes made to the database are written to the disk, and they will persist even if the system is restarted. Durability guarantees that the database will maintain the integrity of committed transactions, providing confidence that once changes are made, they are permanent and will not be lost.

One of the key components of transaction management in relational databases is the transaction log, also known as the redo log or write-ahead log. The transaction log is a record of all the changes made to the database during a transaction, including the data that was modified, the time of the modification, and the identity of the transaction. The transaction log is critical for ensuring durability and providing a mechanism for recovery in the event of a system failure. When a transaction is committed, the changes are first written to the transaction log, and only after the log is updated are the changes applied to the actual database. This ensures that, in the event of a crash, the database can be restored to a consistent state by replaying the transaction log to apply all committed transactions and roll back any incomplete transactions.

In addition to the transaction log, relational databases use locking mechanisms to manage concurrency and ensure that transactions do not interfere with each other. Locks are applied to data items during a transaction to prevent other transactions from accessing or modifying the same data simultaneously. Locks can be applied at different levels, such as row-level locks, page-level locks, or table-level locks, depending on the granularity of the lock and the desired performance. Locking ensures that transactions are isolated from one another and helps prevent conflicts such as lost updates, uncommitted data, and inconsistent reads. However, excessive locking can lead to performance issues, such as deadlocks and contention, where transactions are blocked from accessing the data they need. Therefore, database management systems (DBMS) must balance the need for isolation with the need for performance.

Deadlocks are a common issue in transaction management, and they occur when two or more transactions are waiting for each other to release locks on data, creating a circular dependency that prevents any of the transactions from completing. When a deadlock is detected, the DBMS will automatically choose one of the transactions to be rolled back, allowing the others to proceed. This process is known as deadlock resolution. Deadlocks are often mitigated by using techniques such as lock timeouts, transaction priorities, or by designing the application to access data in a consistent order.

Another important aspect of transaction management is the concept of savepoints, which allow transactions to be partially rolled back to a specific point in time. Savepoints enable users to set intermediate points within a transaction, allowing for finer control over the rollback process. If an error occurs, the transaction can be rolled back to a specific savepoint rather than being fully rolled back, which can improve performance and reduce the impact of errors. Savepoints are particularly useful in complex transactions that involve multiple steps or stages, as they allow for more granular error handling and recovery.

The process of transaction management in relational databases is designed to ensure that databases can handle concurrent access from multiple users and systems while maintaining the integrity and consistency of the data. By enforcing the ACID properties and using techniques such as transaction logs, locks, and savepoints, relational databases can support complex transactional workloads and provide high levels of reliability and performance. Transaction management is a vital component of database systems, particularly in environments where data consistency and reliability are crucial, such as in financial, e-commerce, and healthcare applications. Proper transaction management ensures that even in the face of system failures, power outages, or other unexpected events, the database can recover and maintain the integrity of its data, providing a robust foundation for mission-critical applications.

ACID Properties: Ensuring Transaction Reliability

In relational databases, transactions are essential for maintaining data integrity and consistency, particularly when multiple users or applications are interacting with the database simultaneously. To ensure that transactions are executed reliably, regardless of the number of concurrent operations or system failures, relational database management systems (RDBMS) rely on a set of properties known as ACID. The ACID properties, which stand for Atomicity, Consistency, Isolation, and Durability, provide a framework for guaranteeing the reliability of database transactions. These properties are fundamental for ensuring that a transaction is processed accurately, completely, and without any errors, even in the face of unexpected failures or crashes.

The first of the ACID properties is Atomicity, which is the concept that a transaction must be treated as a single, indivisible unit of work. This means that all operations within the transaction must either be fully completed or fully rolled back, with no partial updates to the database. If any part of a transaction fails, the entire transaction is undone, leaving the database in its initial state. This prevents situations where the database might be left in an inconsistent or incomplete state due to an error, such as only part of a data update being applied or a transaction being interrupted mid-way. Atomicity ensures that the database will never have a situation where some data changes are committed while others are not, which could lead to unreliable results.

For example, consider a bank transfer operation where money is being transferred from one account to another. The transaction involves two operations: deducting the amount from the sender's account and adding it to the recipient's account. If an error occurs after the sender's account has been debited but before the recipient's account is credited, the result would be an inconsistent state where the sender has lost money, but the recipient has not received it. With atomicity, the database ensures that if any part of the transaction fails, both operations are rolled back, and the database is returned to its previous state, leaving no financial discrepancies.

The second ACID property is Consistency, which ensures that a transaction will bring the database from one valid state to another. A valid state means that all predefined integrity constraints, rules, and business logic are maintained. For example, if a database enforces a constraint that an employee's salary must be greater than zero, a transaction that attempts to update the salary to a negative value would be rejected. Consistency guarantees that the transaction will not violate these constraints, and it will preserve the rules defined within the database schema. The database will always maintain its integrity, ensuring that any transaction either succeeds in preserving the consistency of the database or is rolled back entirely if it causes an inconsistency.

For instance, consider a transaction where a customer's order is being processed in an inventory management system. The transaction may involve updating the stock levels in the inventory and recording the sale in the sales database. If the transaction is consistent, the inventory stock will always reflect accurate numbers, and there will be no possibility of negative stock levels or missing records in the sales database. Consistency ensures that the database rules and constraints, such as unique constraints or foreign key relationships, are adhered to, ensuring that no invalid data is written to the system.

Isolation is the third property of ACID, which ensures that transactions are executed in isolation from one another. This means that the operations of one transaction should not interfere with the operations of another, even when they are executed concurrently. Isolation guarantees that each transaction will see a consistent view of the database and will not be impacted by other ongoing transactions. For example, if two transactions are attempting to update the same record simultaneously, isolation ensures that one transaction will be executed completely before the other starts, preventing conflicts like dirty reads, non-repeatable reads, and phantom reads.

Dirty reads occur when a transaction reads data that has been modified by another uncommitted transaction. Non-repeatable reads happen when a transaction reads the same data multiple times, but the data is modified by another transaction between the reads, causing inconsistency in the results. Phantom reads occur when a transaction reads a set of rows that match a certain condition, but another transaction inserts or deletes rows, causing the set of rows to change unexpectedly. To enforce isolation, most relational databases provide different isolation levels, such as READ UNCOMMITTED, READ COMMITTED, REPEATABLE READ, and SERIALIZABLE. These levels control the degree to which transactions can interact with each other, with SERIALIZABLE providing the highest level of isolation, ensuring that no transaction can affect others in any way.

The fourth property, Durability, ensures that once a transaction is committed, its effects are permanent, even in the event of a system failure, power outage, or crash. Once a transaction has been successfully completed, the changes it made to the database are written to stable storage (such as disk), and they will persist, even if the database system crashes immediately after the transaction is committed. This guarantees that once the user is notified that a transaction has been completed, the changes to the database are permanent and will not be lost.

Durability is critical in systems where the accuracy of data is paramount, such as banking systems or e-commerce platforms, where financial transactions and customer information must be preserved without any loss. For example, if a user successfully places an order in an online store, the order should be recorded permanently in the database, even if there is a power failure immediately after the order confirmation. Durability ensures that the database can recover from such failures without losing committed transactions, providing the user and the system with confidence that the data is accurate and secure.

ACID properties are essential for maintaining the reliability and consistency of relational databases, especially in environments where concurrent transactions are frequent, and data integrity is critical. They help ensure that the database can handle multiple operations and users simultaneously, without compromising the accuracy or integrity of the data. The implementation of ACID properties is one of the reasons relational databases have been widely adopted in mission-critical systems where the reliability of data is of utmost importance, such as in financial institutions, healthcare, and e-commerce. By enforcing the guarantees provided by ACID, relational databases provide a robust foundation for supporting business applications and operations that require high levels of data integrity and reliability.

In practice, database management systems achieve the ACID properties using techniques like transaction logs, locking mechanisms, and backup systems. These techniques help ensure that transactions are executed reliably and that the database can recover from any interruptions or failures. While ACID properties provide a strong foundation for transaction management, modern databases also include features such as distributed transactions, multi-version concurrency control (MVCC), and replication to address the challenges posed by larger, more complex systems. These features further enhance the ability of relational databases to maintain data consistency, reliability, and performance in the face of increasing transaction loads and system complexities.

Concurrency Control: Managing Simultaneous Transactions

Concurrency control in relational databases is a crucial concept that ensures the correct execution of simultaneous transactions. In environments where multiple users or applications are accessing and modifying the database concurrently, it is essential to prevent conflicts, ensure data integrity, and maintain a consistent view of the data. When multiple transactions are executing at the same time, there is a risk that they may interfere with each other, leading to issues such as lost updates, inconsistent reads, and violations of data integrity. Concurrency control mechanisms are designed to manage these simultaneous transactions, ensuring that the database remains in a consistent state and that the operations of one transaction do not negatively affect those of another.

One of the primary goals of concurrency control is to provide isolation between transactions. Isolation ensures that each transaction is executed independently and does not interfere with other transactions. In an ideal situation, each transaction should be able to execute as if it were the only transaction in the system, without being affected by other ongoing transactions. However, in real-world systems, it is common for multiple transactions to execute at the same time, which is where concurrency control comes into play. The aim is to allow for parallel execution of transactions while preventing them from causing inconsistencies or conflicts in the database.

To achieve this, database management systems (DBMS) employ various techniques and protocols, including locking mechanisms, transaction isolation levels, and multi-version concurrency control (MVCC). These techniques help control the access to data by multiple transactions, ensuring that they can operate in parallel without violating the ACID properties of transactions. The choice of concurrency control method depends on factors such as the database system's design, the nature of the application, and the level of performance required.

Locking is one of the most commonly used concurrency control techniques. It involves placing locks on the data that a transaction is accessing, preventing other transactions from modifying that data until the lock is released. Locks can be applied at different levels of granularity, such as row-level locks, page-level locks, or table-level locks, depending on the system's needs and the desired performance. Row-level locks are the most granular, locking only the specific row that is being accessed, while table-level locks lock the entire table, preventing other transactions from accessing any rows in the table. While row-level locks allow for higher concurrency and greater performance, they also come with the risk of deadlocks, where two or more transactions are waiting on each other to release locks, creating a cycle of dependencies that prevents any of the transactions from proceeding.

To avoid deadlocks, DBMS use deadlock detection and resolution techniques. When a deadlock occurs, the system identifies the transactions involved in the deadlock and chooses one to roll back, allowing the other transactions to proceed. This process is known as deadlock resolution. Another strategy for preventing deadlocks is to use a lock timeout, where a transaction will automatically abort if it has been waiting for a lock for too long. While locking is effective for ensuring data integrity, it can lead to performance bottlenecks, especially in systems with high transaction volumes or when locks are held for extended periods.

Transaction isolation levels define the degree to which the operations of one transaction are isolated from those of other concurrent transactions. The SQL standard defines four isolation levels, each providing a different balance between concurrency and consistency. These levels are READ UNCOMMITTED, READ COMMITTED, REPEATABLE READ, and SERIALIZABLE. Each level specifies how much data from other transactions can be read or modified during the execution of the current transaction.

The READ UNCOMMITTED isolation level allows transactions to read data that has been modified by other uncommitted transactions, which is known as a dirty read. This level provides the highest concurrency but at the cost of data integrity, as it allows transactions to read inconsistent or intermediate data. READ COMMITTED is the default isolation level for many databases, and it ensures that transactions only read data that has been committed by other transactions, preventing dirty reads. However, it still allows for non-repeatable reads, where the value of a data item can change between two reads within the same transaction if another transaction modifies it.

REPEATABLE READ ensures that once a transaction reads a value, it will see the same value for the duration of the transaction, preventing non-repeatable reads. However, it still allows for phantom reads, where a transaction may see a different set of rows when it repeats a query due to the insertion or deletion of rows by other transactions. The highest level of isolation is SERIALIZABLE, which ensures that transactions are executed in such a way that the results are the same as if they had been executed serially, one after the other, without any overlap. While SERIALIZABLE provides the highest level of data consistency, it can significantly reduce concurrency and impact performance, as it effectively serializes access to the data, preventing simultaneous transactions.

Another concurrency control mechanism used in modern databases is multi-version concurrency control (MVCC). MVCC allows multiple transactions to access different versions of a data item concurrently without blocking each other. Instead of locking data, MVCC creates a new version of the data each time a transaction modifies it, and each transaction operates on its own version of the data. This allows for higher concurrency and improved performance, as transactions can read data without being blocked by other transactions. MVCC is commonly used in databases that require high levels of concurrency, such as PostgreSQL and Oracle. While MVCC improves performance, it also introduces the need for garbage collection and version management to clean up old versions of data that are no longer needed.

Optimistic concurrency control is another technique used to handle concurrent transactions, particularly in systems where conflicts between transactions are rare. In optimistic concurrency control, transactions are allowed to execute without acquiring locks. Instead, the system tracks changes made by each transaction, and at the end of the transaction, it checks whether any conflicts have occurred. If no conflicts are detected, the transaction is committed; if conflicts are found, the transaction is rolled back. This approach minimizes the overhead associated with locking and allows for high concurrency, but it can lead to transaction rollbacks if conflicts occur.

Concurrency control is essential for ensuring that relational databases can handle multiple transactions simultaneously without compromising the integrity of the data. Effective concurrency control allows databases to operate efficiently in multi-user environments, supporting a wide range of applications from financial systems to e-commerce platforms. By balancing the trade-offs between performance and consistency, database management systems can provide high levels of concurrency while ensuring that transactions are executed reliably and accurately. Whether using locking mechanisms, isolation levels, MVCC, or optimistic concurrency control, the goal is always to ensure that data integrity is maintained and that users can trust the results of their transactions, even when operating in a highly concurrent environment.

Database Locks and Their Impact on Transactions

Database locks are a critical component of concurrency control mechanisms in relational database management systems (RDBMS). They ensure that multiple transactions can be executed concurrently without violating the integrity of the database or causing conflicts between transactions. In environments where multiple users or applications are interacting with the database simultaneously, locks are necessary to prevent data inconsistencies that could arise when multiple transactions attempt to modify the same data at the same time. While locks are essential for maintaining data integrity and isolation between transactions, they also come with challenges and potential performance trade-offs that need to be carefully managed.

The primary purpose of database locks is to control access to data during a transaction. When a transaction accesses data, the database management system (DBMS) places a lock on that data to prevent other transactions from modifying it until the first transaction is completed. This helps to ensure that the data remains in a consistent state, even if multiple transactions are attempting to read or write to the same data concurrently. Without locks, transactions could read or modify data that is in the process of being updated by another transaction, leading to inconsistencies such as lost updates, uncommitted data, or dirty reads.

There are different types of locks that can be applied in a database, and the type of lock used can have a significant impact on the performance and concurrency of the system. The most common types of locks are shared locks and exclusive locks. A shared lock allows multiple transactions to read the same data simultaneously, but it prevents any of them from modifying it. This type of lock is typically used for read operations, where the data is being accessed but not changed. An exclusive lock, on the other hand, is placed when a transaction intends to modify data. An exclusive lock prevents any other transactions from either reading or writing the locked data until the transaction holding the lock is completed. Exclusive locks are essential for ensuring that updates to the database are performed safely and consistently.

Locks can be applied at different levels of granularity, depending on the scope of the data being locked. The most granular level of locking is row-level locking, which locks individual rows in a table. Row-level locks allow for higher concurrency, as transactions can modify different rows of the same table simultaneously without interfering with each other. However, row-level locks come with the potential risk of deadlocks, where two or more transactions are waiting for each other to release locks, causing them to be stuck in a cycle of dependencies. A more coarse-grained lock is a table-level lock, which locks the entire table. Table-level locks are typically less efficient because they block access to the entire table, preventing other transactions from reading or modifying any of its rows, even if those transactions are not concerned with the specific rows being updated. While table-level locks can reduce the risk of deadlocks, they significantly limit concurrency and can lead to performance bottlenecks in systems with high transaction volumes.

Lock contention is another important factor to consider when working with database locks. Contention occurs when multiple transactions request access to the same locked data, causing them to wait for the lock to be released. High lock contention can lead to delays in transaction processing, as transactions are forced to wait for the necessary locks to be granted. In systems with high concurrency, lock contention can severely degrade performance, particularly when transactions are long-running or when locks are held for extended periods of time. To minimize lock contention, it is important for database administrators to optimize the design of the database schema, ensure that transactions are as efficient as possible, and use appropriate isolation levels that balance the need for data consistency with the need for concurrency.

Deadlocks are one of the most significant challenges associated with database locks. A deadlock occurs when two or more transactions are waiting for each other to release locks, creating a situation where none of the transactions can proceed. Deadlocks typically arise when transactions acquire locks in different orders, causing a circular dependency where each transaction is holding a lock that another transaction needs. For example, if Transaction A holds a lock on Row 1 and is waiting for a lock on Row 2, while Transaction B holds a lock on Row 2 and is waiting for a lock on Row 1, both transactions are deadlocked and cannot proceed. To resolve deadlocks, most RDBMS have mechanisms in place to detect and resolve them automatically. This typically involves identifying one of the transactions involved in the deadlock and aborting it, allowing the other transactions to proceed. Although deadlock detection and resolution are critical for maintaining the integrity of the database, they can introduce additional overhead, as the system must constantly monitor transactions for potential deadlocks.

The impact of locks on transaction performance and concurrency depends on several factors, including the isolation level, the type of lock used, and the duration of the transaction. Isolation levels define the extent to which transactions are isolated from one another, and they directly influence the type and frequency of locks that are applied. For example, the READ COMMITTED isolation level allows transactions to read only committed data, which typically results in the use of shared locks. However, it also allows for non-repeatable reads, where the data being read may be modified by other transactions before the first transaction is completed. The SERIALIZABLE isolation level, on the other hand, provides the highest level of isolation by ensuring that transactions are executed in a way that is equivalent to running them serially, one after the other. This often results in exclusive locks being applied more frequently, reducing concurrency but ensuring that transactions do not interfere with each other.

One of the primary goals of database management is to strike a balance between ensuring data consistency and maintaining high performance. While locks are essential for ensuring the consistency and reliability of the database, they can also introduce performance bottlenecks if not carefully managed. Optimizing the use of locks requires considering factors such as transaction size, isolation level, and the type of lock applied. For instance, using row-level locks and appropriate isolation levels can help minimize the impact of locks on concurrency while still ensuring that the data remains consistent and isolated. Additionally, designing the database schema with efficient indexing and ensuring that transactions are as short and efficient as possible can help reduce the likelihood of lock contention and deadlocks.

Another important consideration when working with database locks is the impact of long-running transactions. Long-running transactions hold locks for extended periods of time, which increases the likelihood of lock contention and can prevent other transactions from accessing the data they need. To mitigate this issue, database systems can use techniques such as lock timeouts and transaction timeouts, where transactions are automatically rolled back if they exceed a certain duration. This helps prevent transactions from holding locks indefinitely and ensures that the system remains responsive and efficient.

Database locks are an essential tool for managing simultaneous transactions and ensuring the integrity of the data. However, they come with their own set of challenges, including lock contention, deadlocks, and performance bottlenecks. By carefully managing the use of locks, optimizing transaction design, and selecting appropriate isolation levels, database administrators can strike a balance between ensuring data consistency and maintaining high concurrency. Understanding the impact of locks on transactions is crucial for building efficient, scalable, and reliable database systems that can handle the demands of modern applications and business environments.

Isolation Levels and Their Influence on Database Operations

In relational databases, isolation levels play a crucial role in determining how transactions interact with each other and how data consistency is maintained in the face of concurrent transactions. Isolation is one of the ACID properties—Atomicity, Consistency, Isolation, and Durability—that guarantees the reliability and integrity of database operations. While atomicity ensures that transactions are treated as a single unit, and consistency ensures that the database transitions from one valid state to another, isolation defines the extent to which the operations of one transaction are visible to others. It influences how transactions are allowed to interact with each other when they access the same data concurrently, thus affecting performance, data consistency, and the likelihood of encountering issues such as dirty reads, non-repeatable reads, and phantom reads.

The concept of isolation is essential for managing the challenges of concurrency in multi-user or multi-transaction environments. When multiple transactions are running simultaneously, the database must ensure that their operations do not conflict with one another. If isolation is not properly enforced, transactions may interfere with each other, leading to inconsistent or incorrect results. To address these challenges, the SQL standard defines several isolation levels, each offering different trade-offs between data consistency and system performance. The four main isolation levels are READ UNCOMMITTED, READ COMMITTED, REPEATABLE READ, and SERIALIZABLE. Each level defines the rules for how transactions interact and the types of anomalies they are susceptible to.

At the lowest level of isolation, READ UNCOMMITTED allows transactions to read data that has been modified by other transactions but not yet committed. This means that a transaction can read "dirty" data—data that is in an intermediate state and may not reflect the final outcome of the transaction that is modifying it. While this isolation level provides the highest level of concurrency because transactions can freely read and write to the database without being blocked by locks, it comes with significant risks. Dirty reads can result in incorrect or inconsistent data being used for calculations, reporting, or decision-making. For example, if a transaction reads data that is subsequently rolled back, the data it read could be invalid. As a result, READ UNCOMMITTED is typically not recommended for most applications, particularly those that require a high degree of data accuracy and integrity.

READ COMMITTED, the next level of isolation, ensures that transactions can only read data that has been committed by other transactions. In this level, a transaction is prevented from reading dirty data, as it can only access data that has been finalized and committed to the database. While this eliminates the risk of dirty reads, it still allows for another issue known as non-repeatable reads. A non-repeatable read occurs when a transaction reads the same data twice, but the data has been modified by another transaction in between the reads. This can lead to inconsistent results when the data changes after being read, creating potential discrepancies in computations or reports. READ COMMITTED is the default isolation level in many databases, and while it offers better data consistency than READ UNCOMMITTED, it still allows for some level of inconsistency when transactions are concurrently modifying the same data.

REPEATABLE READ, the third isolation level, takes steps to prevent non-repeatable reads by ensuring that once a transaction reads a piece of data, it will see the same value for that data throughout the duration of the transaction. This level of isolation guarantees that no other transaction can modify the data that has been read by the current transaction, preventing the scenario where a transaction sees different values for the same data at different times. However, REPEATABLE READ does not fully eliminate the possibility of anomalies. It still allows for phantom reads, which occur when a transaction retrieves a set of rows that match a condition, but another transaction inserts, updates, or deletes rows that would have matched the condition. As a result, the result set of the query can change between the time it is initially read and the time it is re-read, leading to inconsistent results. REPEATABLE READ provides a stronger guarantee of data consistency than READ COMMITTED, but it still has some limitations in highly concurrent environments.

The highest level of isolation is SERIALIZABLE, which ensures that transactions are executed in such a way that their results are equivalent to if they were run sequentially, one after the other. SERIALIZABLE eliminates the possibility of dirty reads, non-repeatable reads, and phantom reads by enforcing strict control over data access. At this level, the database ensures that the outcome of concurrent transactions is the same as if they were executed in a serial order, with no overlapping or interleaving of operations. This level provides the highest degree of data consistency but at the cost of performance and concurrency. Transactions must wait for locks to be released before they can access the data, which can lead to significant delays in environments with high transaction volumes. SERIALIZABLE is typically used in situations where data integrity is paramount, such as in financial systems or systems that handle critical, real-time data.

The choice of isolation level has a direct impact on both the performance of the database and the integrity of the data. Lower isolation levels, such as READ UNCOMMITTED, allow for higher concurrency but at the expense of data accuracy, as they permit dirty reads and other anomalies. Higher isolation levels, such as SERIALIZABLE, provide stronger guarantees of data consistency but can result in lower performance due to the increased contention for locks and the overhead associated with managing strict isolation between transactions. As a result, the choice of isolation level should be carefully considered based on the specific requirements of the application and the expected workload.

In addition to the impact on performance and consistency, isolation levels also affect the likelihood of encountering deadlocks. A deadlock occurs when two or more transactions are waiting for each other to release locks on the same data, resulting in a situation where none of the transactions can proceed. Deadlocks are more likely to occur at higher isolation levels, particularly in systems with high transaction volumes or complex queries. Deadlock detection and resolution mechanisms are used by most DBMS to automatically detect and resolve deadlocks, but they can introduce additional overhead to the system. As such, careful management of isolation levels and transaction design is essential for minimizing deadlocks and optimizing the performance of the database.

One way to mitigate the performance impact of higher isolation levels is by using techniques such as optimistic concurrency control, which allows transactions to execute without acquiring locks initially and only checks for conflicts at the end of the transaction. This approach is particularly useful in systems where conflicts between transactions are rare and helps to strike a balance between performance and data consistency.

Isolation levels are a critical tool for managing the trade-offs between data consistency and system performance in relational databases. By carefully selecting the appropriate isolation level, database administrators and application developers can control the level of concurrency allowed and ensure that transactions operate reliably and consistently. The choice of isolation level depends on factors such as the nature of the data, the type of application, and the level of performance required. Understanding the influence of isolation levels on database operations is essential for designing efficient, scalable, and reliable database systems that meet the needs of modern applications.

Rollbacks and Recovery Mechanisms in Relational Databases

Rollbacks and recovery mechanisms are essential components in ensuring the reliability and integrity of relational databases. They provide a safety net to protect the database from errors, failures, or unintended consequences of transactions, allowing the system to revert to a consistent state. These mechanisms are critical for maintaining the ACID properties of relational databases, particularly Atomicity, Consistency, and Durability. When a transaction encounters an issue or when the system experiences a failure, rollbacks and recovery mechanisms ensure that the database can recover gracefully, restoring the database to a valid state and ensuring that no data is lost or corrupted in the process.

A rollback occurs when a transaction cannot be completed successfully, and the database needs to be returned to its previous state before the transaction began. The primary reason for a rollback is the violation of one or more constraints or business rules during the transaction. For example, if a transaction is attempting to update a record in the database and the new data violates a foreign key constraint or attempts to insert invalid data, the database system will abort the transaction and roll back any changes made so far. This process ensures that partial changes to the database are not committed, preventing the database from ending up in an inconsistent or invalid state. Rollbacks help to maintain the integrity of the data by ensuring that only fully completed transactions are reflected in the database.

In relational databases, the ability to perform a rollback relies on the use of transaction logs, which record every change made to the database during the course of a transaction. These logs are essential for both performing rollbacks and supporting recovery mechanisms.

When a transaction begins, all changes made to the data are first written to the transaction log before being applied to the database. If a transaction is successful and is committed, the changes are permanently written to the database. However, if an error occurs, or if the transaction is explicitly rolled back, the database can refer to the transaction log to undo the changes. This rollback process ensures that the database is returned to the state it was in before the transaction began, preserving data consistency and preventing any inconsistencies or corruption caused by partial updates.

While rollbacks handle the situation when a transaction fails or is manually aborted, recovery mechanisms are designed to handle system failures, such as power outages, crashes, or other unexpected disruptions that could cause the database to become inconsistent. Recovery mechanisms ensure that, after such a failure, the database can restore its previous state and resume normal operations without losing data. In order to implement recovery mechanisms effectively, most relational database systems use a combination of transaction logs, checkpoints, and write-ahead logging techniques.

Transaction logs, also known as redo logs or write-ahead logs, play a pivotal role in both rollbacks and recovery. These logs capture every change made to the database during a transaction, including data modifications and metadata updates. The transaction log records both the original data before it is modified (for undo purposes) and the new data after the modification (for redo purposes). This allows the database to not only roll back uncommitted changes but also recover changes made by committed transactions in the event of a crash. The transaction log is crucial in ensuring that no data is lost during a failure, as it provides a detailed record of all operations performed on the database.

Checkpoints are another key component of recovery mechanisms. A checkpoint is a point in time where the database commits all changes made so far and synchronizes the transaction log with the data files. By periodically creating checkpoints, the database can reduce the amount of work required during recovery. If a failure occurs, the system can recover the database to the most recent checkpoint and then replay the transaction log from that point onward to apply any changes made after the checkpoint. This minimizes the amount of data that needs to be reprocessed during recovery and helps speed up the recovery process.

In addition to transaction logs and checkpoints, write-ahead logging (WAL) is a technique used in many relational databases to ensure data integrity during recovery. WAL requires that before any changes are written to the database, they must first be recorded in the transaction log. This ensures that the database can always recover from a failure, as all changes are first captured in the log before being applied to the data files. By adhering to the WAL principle, the database ensures that in the event of a crash, it can either roll back uncommitted transactions or replay committed transactions from the log to restore the database to a consistent state.

Another important aspect of recovery mechanisms is the concept of consistent snapshots. During normal operation, the database may take periodic snapshots or backups of its data. These snapshots capture the state of the database at a particular point in time and serve as a restore point in the event of catastrophic failure. Backup strategies can vary from full backups, which capture the entire database, to incremental backups, which capture only the changes since the last backup. In case of a failure, the database can be restored from the most recent backup, and the transaction log can be applied to bring the database up to date with the latest changes made before the failure. This ensures that the recovery process can be completed quickly, with minimal data loss.

The recovery process after a failure generally follows a series of steps. First, the database system restores the most recent backup, if available. Then, it applies the transaction log to recover any changes that were made after the backup was taken. Finally, the database checks for incomplete transactions and either rolls them back or commits them, depending on the state recorded in the transaction log. This process ensures that the database is restored to a consistent state, with all changes either fully applied or fully undone, depending on their status at the time of the failure.

While transaction logs, checkpoints, and write-ahead logging are essential for ensuring data recovery, the efficiency of recovery mechanisms depends on how well the database handles logging and checkpoints. In systems with heavy transaction loads or high availability requirements, recovery times can become a significant factor. To minimize downtime and improve recovery performance, database administrators may implement strategies such as log shipping, replication, or clustering, which help distribute the load and improve the fault tolerance of the database system. By ensuring that data is replicated across multiple nodes or servers, these strategies can provide additional redundancy and enable faster recovery times in case of failure.

The ability to roll back transactions and recover from failures is vital for maintaining the integrity and availability of relational databases. These mechanisms ensure that transactions are executed reliably, even in the face of errors or system crashes, and that data remains consistent and accurate. Through the use of transaction logs, checkpoints, write-ahead logging, and backup strategies, relational databases can offer robust recovery solutions that support high levels of data reliability and availability. Rollbacks and recovery mechanisms are foundational to the smooth operation of any database system, ensuring that businesses and applications can continue to rely on their data even in the event of unexpected disruptions.

Relational Database Indexing: A Performance Booster

Relational database indexing is a fundamental technique used to optimize the performance of query processing. As databases grow in size and complexity, querying the data efficiently becomes increasingly important. Indexing is a mechanism that improves the speed of data retrieval operations, particularly for large datasets where searching through each record sequentially would be too slow. By creating indexes, databases can access data more quickly and reduce the time required for queries, thereby enhancing overall system performance. Although indexes can significantly speed up query performance, they also introduce some trade-offs, such as increased storage requirements and potential overhead during data modification operations.

At its core, an index in a relational database is a data structure that stores a sorted list of values from one or more columns in a table, along with pointers to the corresponding rows in the table. Indexes are similar to the index in a book, where you can quickly find the page number associated with a particular keyword. In a database, indexes enable the system to locate specific rows based on the indexed columns without having to scan the entire table. This can drastically improve the performance of search queries, especially those that involve filtering, sorting, or joining tables.

The most commonly used type of index is the B-tree index, which organizes data in a balanced tree structure. In a B-tree index, each node contains a range of values, and the tree is structured in such a way that it allows for fast traversal to find the desired value. B-trees are efficient for a wide range of query types, including range queries, equality queries, and sorting operations. As a result, most relational databases, including MySQL, PostgreSQL, and Oracle, use B-trees or variations of them as their default indexing method. The B-tree index ensures that the database engine can quickly find the location of a value by traversing the tree from the root to the leaf nodes in logarithmic time, making it highly efficient even for large datasets.

Another type of index is the hash index, which is used for equality comparisons, particularly in situations where the query involves looking for an exact match of a value. In a hash index, a hash function is applied to the indexed column, and the result is used to determine the location of the data in the table. Hash indexes are very efficient for finding exact matches, but they are not suitable for range queries or sorting operations because the values are not stored in any particular order. Therefore, hash indexes are typically used for specific types of queries where performance is critical, such as searching for a specific value in a large dataset.

Full-text indexing is another variant, commonly used for searching large text fields, such as in content management systems or search engines. Full-text indexes create a special type of index that allows for efficient searching of words and phrases within text columns. These indexes are particularly useful when performing searches on unstructured data or large documents. Unlike traditional indexes that search for exact values, full-text indexes allow for more complex querying, such as finding all records containing a particular word or phrase, or even ranking results based on relevance.

Creating indexes can improve the performance of read operations significantly, but it also introduces some trade-offs, particularly with respect to write operations. When a table has indexes, any INSERT, UPDATE, or DELETE operation must also update the indexes to reflect the changes in the table. This overhead can slow down write operations, especially if there are multiple indexes on the same table. As a result, database administrators must carefully balance the need for fast read performance with the overhead of maintaining indexes during write operations. In scenarios where write performance is critical, it may be necessary to limit the number of indexes on a table or use indexing strategies that reduce the impact on write performance.

Moreover, indexes consume additional disk space, which can be a consideration when dealing with very large datasets or when storage resources are limited. While B-tree indexes and hash indexes are relatively efficient in terms of storage, full-text indexes and other specialized index types can require significant amounts of space, especially if the indexed data is large or highly variable. Therefore, the benefits of indexing must be weighed against the storage costs, and unnecessary or redundant indexes should be avoided.

The choice of which columns to index is a critical decision in database optimization. Indexing every column in a table is generally not a good idea, as it can lead to excessive overhead and storage requirements. Instead, indexes should be created on columns that are frequently used in query conditions, such as columns involved in WHERE clauses, JOIN conditions, or ORDER BY clauses. For example, in a table of customer information, indexing columns like "customer_id" or "email" may be beneficial, as these are commonly queried for lookups or updates. However, indexing columns that are rarely used in queries or that have low cardinality (i.e., columns with only a few distinct values) may not provide a significant performance benefit and may add unnecessary overhead.

Composite indexes, which combine multiple columns into a single index, are another useful optimization strategy. A composite index can improve the performance of queries that filter or sort based on multiple columns simultaneously. For example, if a query often filters based on both "first_name" and "last_name," creating a composite index on these two columns can make the query more efficient. However, the order of columns in a composite index is important—queries that filter on the leftmost columns in the index will benefit the most from it. As such, composite indexes should be created with careful consideration of the most common query patterns.

One challenge with indexing is maintaining the indexes over time as the data in the database changes. As records are inserted, updated, or deleted, the index must be kept in sync with the changes in the table. In cases where there is frequent modification of the indexed columns, the overhead of maintaining the indexes can become a performance bottleneck. To address this issue, some databases support indexing strategies that optimize the performance of frequently updated tables, such as partial indexes, which index only a subset of the rows based on a specified condition, or covering indexes, which include all the columns needed by a query in the index itself, thus reducing the need for additional lookups in the table.

Another consideration when using indexes is the potential for index fragmentation, which occurs when the data in the index becomes disorganized due to frequent updates, deletes, or inserts. Fragmentation can lead to performance degradation because the database engine has to work harder to traverse the index and locate the data. Regular maintenance, such as index rebuilding or reorganizing, can help mitigate fragmentation and maintain optimal performance. Most modern database systems provide automated tools or commands to rebuild or reorganize indexes as needed.

Indexes are an essential tool for improving the performance of relational databases, enabling fast data retrieval even for large datasets. By creating the right indexes on frequently queried columns and using appropriate index types, database administrators can significantly enhance query performance. However, indexing requires careful management to balance the benefits of faster reads with the overhead of slower writes and increased storage requirements. By understanding the impact of indexing on database performance and continuously monitoring and optimizing indexes, relational databases can be fine-tuned to provide high performance and scalability for modern applications.

Types of Indexes and Their Use Cases

Indexes are crucial components of relational databases that significantly enhance query performance by improving data retrieval speeds. They serve as lookup tables for quickly finding records in a database, similar to an index in a book that allows readers to quickly find information without having to read through every page. Indexing is especially important for large datasets where scanning each record in a table would be inefficient. While indexing offers substantial performance improvements, it also comes with trade-offs in terms of storage requirements and the performance impact on write operations. The types of indexes available in relational databases vary, each suited for specific use cases based on the query patterns and data characteristics.

The most common type of index is the B-tree index, which is used by many relational database management systems (RDBMS) as the default indexing method. The B-tree index is a balanced tree structure, where each node contains a range of values, and the tree allows for efficient searching, inserting, and deleting operations. B-trees are particularly useful for queries that involve range searches, equality queries, and sorting. A B-tree index maintains a sorted order of values, which allows for quick retrieval of data. For example, if you need to find all records where a certain column falls within a specific range, a B-tree index will provide a quick way to locate those records without scanning the entire table. B-tree indexes are highly efficient for most general-purpose querying and are widely used in databases such as MySQL, PostgreSQL, and Oracle.

However, B-tree indexes are not always the most efficient option for all types of queries. When the query pattern involves checking for exact matches on a column, such as looking up a specific value, a hash index may be a more appropriate choice. A hash index uses a hash function to convert the indexed column's value into a fixed-size hash value, which is then used to locate the corresponding data in the table. Hash indexes are particularly efficient for equality-based searches, such as finding records that match a specific key value. Because hash indexes are designed for exact matches, they are not well-suited for range queries or sorting operations. When an application requires quick lookups of individual values, such as when searching for a customer ID or a product code, hash indexes can provide significant performance improvements over B-tree indexes.

In addition to B-trees and hash indexes, there are also full-text indexes, which are used primarily for text-based searches. Full-text indexing is used to index large text fields, such as product descriptions, blog posts, or customer reviews. Full-text indexes create a specialized index that allows for fast searching of individual words or phrases within large text columns. Unlike traditional indexes that search for exact matches, full-text indexes enable more advanced search capabilities, such as finding all records that contain a specific word or ranking results by relevance. Full-text indexing is commonly used in content management systems, search engines, and applications that involve searching large text-based datasets. The key advantage of full-text indexing is that it supports complex search queries, such as partial matches, phrase searches, and boolean logic (AND, OR, NOT), which are essential for building advanced search functionality.

Another type of index is the composite index, which combines multiple columns into a single index. A composite index is useful when queries involve conditions on multiple columns. By indexing more than one column together, the database can efficiently process queries that filter or sort on multiple attributes. For example, if a query filters by both a customer's first name and last name, a composite index on both columns will improve performance. The order of columns in a composite index is important, as it affects the index's ability to optimize queries. The most selective columns (those with the fewest distinct values) should typically be placed first in the composite index. Composite indexes are ideal when queries frequently use multiple columns together in WHERE clauses or for sorting, as they allow for faster data retrieval without needing multiple indexes for each individual column.

Bitmap indexes are another specialized index type that is used when a table has low cardinality, meaning the column being indexed has only a few distinct values. Bitmap indexes use a bitmap, which is a bit array where each bit represents the presence or absence of a value for a specific record. This type of index is particularly useful for columns with a small number of unique values, such as gender, status flags (active/inactive), or categories. Bitmap indexes are highly efficient for operations like AND, OR, and NOT, as the database can quickly combine the bitmaps of multiple columns to evaluate the conditions. While bitmap indexes provide excellent performance for certain types of queries, they are not well-suited for columns with high cardinality or for tables with frequent updates, as modifying the bitmap structure can be expensive. Bitmap indexes are typically used in data warehousing and analytical applications, where read-heavy workloads are common.

Spatial indexes are used for indexing spatial data, such as geographic locations, points, and shapes. These indexes are essential for applications that deal with geographic information systems (GIS), such as mapping services or location-based apps. Spatial indexing methods, such as the R-tree index, organize spatial data in a way that allows for efficient querying of geometric shapes and spatial relationships. R-trees, for example, divide the space into bounding boxes and allow for efficient searches that involve spatial relationships like "contains," "intersects," or "within." Spatial indexes are crucial when working with large-scale datasets of geographic data, as they enable fast proximity searches and help to efficiently handle complex spatial queries.

While indexing provides significant benefits in terms of query performance, it also introduces trade-offs that must be carefully managed. One of the main trade-offs is the impact of indexing on write operations. When data is inserted, updated, or deleted, the indexes associated with the affected columns must also be updated, which can introduce overhead and slow down write operations. As the number of indexes on a table increases, so does the time required to maintain them during write operations. Therefore, database administrators must carefully evaluate which columns to index and ensure that indexes are used effectively without negatively impacting the performance of write-heavy workloads. Additionally, indexes consume disk space, which can become a consideration when dealing with large databases or when working in environments with limited storage capacity. The storage overhead introduced by indexes must be balanced against the performance benefits they provide.

Another challenge with indexes is maintaining them over time. As data is modified, indexes can become fragmented, leading to reduced performance. Fragmentation occurs when data is added, deleted, or updated in such a way that the index becomes disordered or inefficient. To mitigate fragmentation, many databases offer maintenance features such as index rebuilding or reorganization, which help restore the efficiency of the indexes. Regular index maintenance is crucial for ensuring that indexes continue to provide optimal performance as the database grows and evolves.

Indexes are essential tools for improving the performance of relational databases, enabling faster data retrieval and more efficient query processing. Different types of indexes, such as B-trees, hash indexes, full-text indexes, composite indexes, bitmap indexes, and spatial indexes, are suited for different use cases depending on the query patterns and data characteristics. While indexes can significantly enhance query performance, they also come with trade-offs, such as increased storage requirements and potential overhead during write operations. By understanding the various types of indexes and their use cases, database administrators can design efficient indexing strategies that balance the need for performance with the costs associated with indexing, ensuring that relational databases perform optimally for a wide range of applications.

Joins and Their Role in Relational Database Queries

In relational databases, joins play a central role in combining data from multiple tables to provide comprehensive results for complex queries. Relational databases typically organize data into separate tables, each storing information related to a specific entity. For example, a database may have one table for customers, another for orders, and another for products. However, real-world data often requires the retrieval of related information from multiple tables simultaneously. Joins are the mechanism that relational database management systems (RDBMS) use to combine these tables in a meaningful way, enabling users to run queries that involve multiple sources of data.

The primary purpose of a join is to establish a relationship between two or more tables based on a common field, often referred to as a key. This key is usually a primary key in one table and a foreign key in another. For instance, an order table may contain a foreign key that references the customer table's primary key, allowing the database to associate each order with a specific customer. Joins allow the database to match rows in one table with corresponding rows in another based on these key relationships. By doing so, joins help to provide a complete set of information from multiple sources, ensuring that the query results reflect all relevant data.

The most common type of join is the INNER JOIN, which returns only the rows where there is a match in both tables. When two tables are joined using an INNER JOIN, the database will only include the records that have corresponding values in both tables based on the specified join condition. For example, if you wanted to retrieve a list of customers along with their orders, you would use an INNER JOIN to match rows from the customer table with those from the order table, where the customer ID field in both tables is equal. The result will only include customers who have placed orders. Any customers without orders or orders without a corresponding customer would be excluded. The INNER JOIN is one of the most frequently used joins in relational database queries due to its ability to filter data efficiently.

While INNER JOIN is widely used, there are other types of joins that serve different purposes and are useful in various situations. One such join is the LEFT JOIN, also known as LEFT OUTER JOIN. A LEFT JOIN returns all rows from the left table, along with the matching rows from the right table. If there is no match, the result will contain NULL values for columns from the right table. This type of join is particularly useful when you want to retrieve all records from one table, regardless of whether they have a corresponding match in another table. For instance, if you wanted to list all customers and any orders they may have placed, you could use a LEFT JOIN to include customers without any orders. For these customers, the order-related columns in the result would contain NULL values, indicating that no matching records were found in the order table.

Similarly, the RIGHT JOIN, or RIGHT OUTER JOIN, works in the opposite way. It returns all rows from the right table, along with matching rows from the left table. If there is no corresponding match in the left table, NULL values are returned for the left table's columns. RIGHT JOIN is less commonly used than LEFT JOIN, but it is still useful when you want to include all rows from the right table in a query result. The key difference between the LEFT JOIN and RIGHT JOIN is the table from which all rows are returned. While the LEFT JOIN returns all rows from the left table, the RIGHT JOIN returns all rows from the right table.

FULL OUTER JOIN is another important type of join. It combines the results of both LEFT JOIN and RIGHT JOIN, returning all rows from both tables. Where there is no match, NULL values are included in the result for the missing side of the join. FULL OUTER JOIN is useful when you need a comprehensive list of records from both tables, regardless of whether there is a match between them. This type of join can be particularly beneficial when combining data from multiple sources, where some data might not have corresponding matches in another source. It ensures that no information is excluded from the result due to missing relationships.

CROSS JOIN is a unique type of join that produces a Cartesian product of the two tables being joined. It returns all possible combinations of rows from both tables, where each row from the first table is paired with every row from the second table. CROSS JOIN does not require a join condition and is typically used in scenarios where such combinations are needed, such as when generating all possible combinations of items or when performing complex analytical calculations. However, because CROSS JOIN can result in very large result sets, it should be used with caution, particularly when dealing with large tables, as it can significantly impact performance and lead to excessive data retrieval.

Joins also have a significant impact on the performance of relational database queries. The more tables involved in a join, the more complex and resource-intensive the operation becomes. When performing a join, the database must match rows from one table with those in another, which can result in considerable computation, especially for large datasets. The complexity of the join operation can increase exponentially as more tables are added. Therefore, it is important to design database queries carefully and optimize the use of joins, particularly in cases where joins are performed on large tables or involve multiple joins. Proper indexing of the columns used in join conditions can significantly improve performance by allowing the database to quickly locate and retrieve the relevant rows.

Another factor that influences the performance of joins is the choice of join type. While INNER JOIN is the most efficient for filtering results, LEFT JOIN and FULL OUTER JOIN may require additional processing time due to the need to handle missing matches and return NULL values for unmatched rows. This can be particularly noticeable when dealing with large datasets or complex queries. Optimizing queries that involve joins requires balancing the need for comprehensive results with the need to minimize query execution time. In some cases, breaking a complex query with multiple joins into smaller subqueries or using temporary tables can help reduce the processing time and improve performance.

The role of joins in relational database queries is indispensable for combining related data from different tables and providing users with meaningful insights. Joins enable relational databases to model complex relationships between entities and present the data in a way that reflects real-world connections. Whether using INNER JOIN to filter results or LEFT JOIN to include unmatched records, joins allow for flexibility and power in querying relational databases. However, they also require careful consideration of performance, especially when working with large datasets or complex queries. Properly optimizing joins is crucial for ensuring that database queries return accurate results efficiently, supporting applications that rely on fast data retrieval and real-time decision-making. Understanding the various types of joins and their role in relational database queries is essential for anyone looking to design effective and efficient database systems.

Subqueries: Nested Queries for Complex Data Retrieval

In relational databases, subqueries are a powerful tool used to perform complex data retrieval operations. A subquery, also known as a nested query or inner query, is a query embedded within another query, typically used to retrieve data that is used as a condition for the outer query. This method allows for more dynamic and flexible data retrieval, enabling users to break down complex queries into manageable components. Subqueries can be placed in various parts of a SQL statement, such as the SELECT, FROM, WHERE, or HAVING clauses, depending on the context and the needs of the query. By allowing queries to be nested within one another, subqueries help streamline the process of extracting meaningful insights from a relational database, particularly when dealing with multiple tables and complex relationships.

One of the most common uses of subqueries is within the WHERE clause, where the result of the subquery is used as a condition for filtering the rows of the outer query. For example, imagine a scenario where a company wants to find employees who work in departments with more than ten employees. Instead of manually querying for the department sizes and then finding the employees who belong to those departments, a subquery can be used to dynamically calculate the number of employees in each department. The outer query can then use this result to filter out the departments with fewer than ten employees, returning only those employees who work in larger departments. By embedding this logic in a single query, subqueries allow for more efficient and concise data retrieval.

Subqueries can also be used in the SELECT clause to perform calculations or return a value that will be included in the result set. This type of subquery is often referred to as a scalar subquery because it returns a single value. For example, if a company wanted to know the average salary of employees in each department, a scalar subquery could be used to calculate the average salary for each department and then display that value alongside the department name in the outer query's results. Scalar subqueries are particularly useful when there is a need to return aggregated or calculated values alongside the original data in the result set, allowing for a more comprehensive view of the data in a single query.

Another common use of subqueries is in the FROM clause, where they can be treated as temporary tables or derived tables. This is particularly useful when working with complex joins or aggregations. By using a subquery in the FROM clause, you can first compute a result set and then use it as a table for further operations in the outer query. This allows for the creation of intermediate result sets that can be joined, filtered, or aggregated without needing to create permanent tables in the database. For example, if you wanted to analyze sales data from multiple regions and compare it against national averages, you could use a subquery in the FROM clause to calculate the sales for each region and then join this result set with other tables to perform further analysis.

Subqueries are not limited to returning single values or result sets; they can also be used in combination with various operators, such as IN, EXISTS, and ALL. The IN operator is often used with subqueries to filter results based on a list of values returned by the subquery. For instance, if you wanted to find all employees whose department IDs matched those of the top-performing departments, you could use a subquery to first identify the department IDs of top performers and then use the IN operator in the outer query to filter employees based on those department IDs. Similarly, the EXISTS operator is used with subqueries to check whether a particular condition holds true for any rows returned by the subquery. The EXISTS operator returns true if the subquery returns one or more rows and false if no rows are returned. This makes it useful for checking the existence of related data in another table, such as finding customers who have placed orders without having to retrieve the actual order details.

Subqueries can also be used in combination with aggregate functions to compute summaries and groupings of data. For example, you can use a subquery to calculate the total sales for each salesperson and then use this result in the outer query to find the salespeople who exceed a certain sales threshold. The combination of subqueries and aggregate functions allows for sophisticated data analysis within a single query, enabling users to perform complex filtering and summarization without the need for multiple queries or intermediate processing steps.

While subqueries provide significant flexibility and power in querying relational databases, they can also introduce performance challenges, particularly when working with large datasets or deeply nested queries. Subqueries, especially those that return large result sets or require multiple levels of nesting, can slow down query performance, as the database must execute the inner query for each row in the outer query. This can result in inefficiencies, particularly when the subquery is executed multiple times, or when it operates on large tables with many rows. In such cases, optimizing the subquery or rethinking the query structure to avoid unnecessary nesting can help improve performance.

One common optimization technique is to use joins instead of subqueries when possible. In many cases, joins can achieve the same result as a subquery, but they tend to be more efficient because they allow the database to retrieve and combine data in a single operation rather than performing multiple nested queries. Joins are typically faster than subqueries because they allow the database engine to utilize indexing and other optimization techniques that are not available with subqueries. However, while joins are often preferred for performance reasons, subqueries remain a useful tool when the query logic is inherently complex or when working with situations where a join would not be appropriate.

Another optimization strategy is to use correlated subqueries, which reference columns from the outer query within the inner query. Correlated subqueries can be more efficient than non-correlated subqueries in certain scenarios because the database only needs to execute the inner query once per row in the outer query, rather than executing the subquery independently for each row. This can reduce the overall processing time of the query, especially when the subquery is relatively simple and the dataset is large.

Subqueries are a powerful and versatile tool in relational database queries, providing a way to handle complex data retrieval, aggregation, and filtering operations within a single query. Whether used to filter data, calculate aggregated values, or create derived tables, subqueries enable users to perform sophisticated operations without the need for multiple queries or additional processing. Despite the potential performance trade-offs, subqueries remain an essential feature of SQL, and their use cases are crucial in creating efficient and effective queries that can handle a wide range of complex data retrieval scenarios. Understanding the various types of subqueries and their role in SQL queries is critical for anyone working with relational databases, as it allows for more efficient, flexible, and powerful data analysis and management.

Data Redundancy and How to Avoid It in Database Design

Data redundancy in a database refers to the unnecessary repetition of the same data across multiple places. While redundancy may seem harmless in small databases, as the system grows and data volume increases, it can lead to inefficiencies, inconsistencies, and difficulties in managing and maintaining the database. Redundant data can result in higher storage costs, slower performance, and problems with data integrity, particularly in environments where data is updated frequently. Thus, avoiding data redundancy is a key goal in database design, ensuring that the database is efficient, maintainable, and reliable.

One of the primary causes of data redundancy is poor database normalization. Normalization is the process of organizing a database's tables and relationships to reduce duplication and ensure that each piece of data is stored only once. The normalization process involves breaking down larger, more complex tables into smaller, more manageable ones, with each table representing a single entity and its attributes. By doing so, normalization helps eliminate repetitive data and ensures that relationships between different entities are accurately represented.

The process of normalization follows a set of rules known as normal forms, which progressively refine the design of the database to eliminate different types of redundancy. The first normal form (1NF) requires that each column in a table contains atomic values, meaning that each value must be indivisible. This ensures that there are no repeating groups or multiple values stored in a single column, which is a common cause of redundancy. The second normal form (2NF) goes further by ensuring that all non-key attributes in a table are fully dependent on the entire primary key, thus eliminating partial dependency and reducing redundancy. The third normal form (3NF) eliminates transitive dependencies, where non-key attributes depend on other non-key attributes, further reducing redundancy. Higher normal forms, such as Boyce-Codd normal form (BCNF) and fourth normal form (4NF), continue to refine the design by eliminating more complex forms of redundancy.

While normalization helps eliminate redundancy, it also introduces the need for foreign keys to represent relationships between tables. Foreign keys are used to link related tables and enforce referential integrity, ensuring that data in one table corresponds to data in another. However, excessive normalization or overuse of foreign keys can sometimes make the database design more complex and harder to manage, especially when the system requires frequent updates or when performance is a concern. It is important to strike a balance between normalization and performance, ensuring that the database is both efficient and flexible.

In some cases, denormalization may be used strategically to improve performance. Denormalization is the process of deliberately introducing some level of redundancy into a database in order to optimize query performance. While denormalization can improve the speed of data retrieval by reducing the number of joins required in complex queries, it also reintroduces the risk of data inconsistency and maintenance challenges. In high-performance systems where speed is critical, denormalization may be necessary, but it should be used judiciously and only in situations where the performance gains outweigh the risks associated with redundancy.

Another technique for avoiding redundancy in database design is the use of unique constraints and indexes. Unique constraints enforce the rule that certain columns must contain unique values, preventing the duplication of data in those columns. For example, in a customer database, an email address column may be constrained to ensure that no two customers can have the same email address. By enforcing uniqueness, the database ensures that redundant data is not accidentally inserted. Similarly, indexes can be used to optimize the performance of queries that filter or sort on specific columns, reducing the need for repetitive data storage while ensuring quick access to the necessary information.

The use of proper relationships between tables also plays a critical role in avoiding redundancy. One-to-many relationships are particularly important in relational databases, where one record in a table can be associated with many records in another table. For example, a single customer can place many orders, and each order will correspond to one customer. Instead of storing customer information in every order record, the database can use a foreign key to associate the order with the customer. This approach minimizes redundancy and ensures that customer data is maintained in only one place, reducing the risk of inconsistent updates or deletion.

Ensuring data integrity is another important consideration in avoiding redundancy. When data is duplicated across multiple tables or records, it becomes more difficult to maintain consistent and accurate information. For example, if an employee's contact information is stored in multiple tables, any updates to their contact details will need to be made in each table. If one of the tables is overlooked during the update process, the data will become inconsistent, leading to potential errors and confusion. By organizing the data properly, using normalization techniques and enforcing foreign key relationships, redundancy is minimized, and data integrity is maintained.

One common scenario where redundancy is introduced is during the process of data import or integration. When data is imported from external sources, such as third-party applications or systems, there may be duplicate records or inconsistencies in the imported data. To avoid redundancy in this scenario, it is important to implement proper data validation and cleansing processes before the data is loaded into the database. These processes can identify duplicate records, correct inconsistencies, and ensure that the imported data adheres to the database's constraints and structure. Regular audits of the database can also help identify and eliminate any redundant data that may have been introduced over time.

Effective data redundancy management also involves monitoring the database over time and continuously optimizing its design as the data evolves. As business needs change and the volume of data grows, the original database design may become less efficient, leading to increased redundancy or performance bottlenecks. Regular database maintenance tasks, such as index optimization, archiving old data, and reorganizing tables, can help ensure that the database remains efficient and free from unnecessary duplication. Additionally, as new use cases or applications are developed, it may be necessary to revisit the database schema and adjust the normalization levels or introduce denormalization to support new requirements.

Redundancy is not always avoidable in some specialized use cases, particularly when it comes to reporting or analytics systems. In data warehousing environments, denormalization is often used to simplify complex queries and reduce the time spent performing joins on large datasets. However, even in these scenarios, it is crucial to strike the right balance between performance and data consistency. By using techniques such as materialized views, indexed views, or summary tables, databases can reduce redundancy while still supporting efficient query performance.

The management of data redundancy is a central aspect of relational database design, impacting both the performance and integrity of the system. By understanding the principles of normalization, carefully considering when and how to use denormalization, and implementing proper relationships and constraints, database designers can minimize redundancy and ensure that the database operates efficiently. As data grows and systems evolve, it is essential to regularly reassess the database design to ensure it continues to meet the needs of the organization while avoiding unnecessary duplication and maintaining high levels of performance.

Optimizing SQL Queries for Better Performance

SQL queries are essential for extracting, updating, and managing data in relational databases. However, as databases grow in size and complexity, ensuring that queries execute efficiently becomes increasingly important. Poorly written or unoptimized queries can result in slow performance, high resource consumption, and bottlenecks that affect the overall system's responsiveness. Optimizing SQL queries is not only a matter of improving speed but also of ensuring that database operations are efficient, reliable, and scalable. The process of query optimization involves analyzing and refining SQL queries to minimize unnecessary processing, reduce the amount of data handled, and improve execution times.

One of the most effective ways to optimize SQL queries is to focus on the structure of the query itself. SQL is a declarative language, meaning that the user specifies what data is needed, not how to retrieve it. However, SQL databases must figure out the most efficient way to execute a query. The database's query planner or optimizer decides on the best execution plan based on the query's structure, indexes, available resources, and other factors. As such, writing efficient SQL code is critical for ensuring that the database can execute queries quickly. For example, selecting only the necessary columns rather than using SELECT * can significantly reduce the amount of data processed by the query. This simple adjustment eliminates unnecessary retrieval of columns that are not required for the task at hand, improving performance by reducing the data volume the database needs to handle.

Proper indexing is another cornerstone of query optimization. Indexes are data structures that improve the speed of data retrieval operations by providing faster access paths to rows in a table. When creating indexes, it is important to focus on the columns that are frequently used in WHERE clauses, JOIN conditions, or ORDER BY clauses. Indexing these columns ensures that the database can quickly locate the relevant rows without scanning the entire table. However, over-indexing can lead to performance issues, as the database needs to update indexes whenever data is inserted, updated, or deleted. Therefore, indexing should be applied selectively, taking into account the specific needs of the application and query patterns. Additionally, it is important to consider the type of index being used. For example, a B-tree index is ideal for most common queries, but specialized indexes such as hash indexes, full-text indexes, or spatial indexes may be more appropriate for specific query types.

Another important aspect of SQL optimization is minimizing the use of subqueries when possible. Subqueries are useful for embedding one query within another, but they can be inefficient, particularly when the subquery is executed multiple times for each row of the outer query. This redundancy can lead to unnecessary computation, especially for large datasets. In many cases, replacing subqueries with JOINs can lead to better performance. Joins allow the database to process the data in a more streamlined manner by directly combining tables based on common keys, rather than running a separate query for each match. While subqueries can sometimes be necessary for complex scenarios, simplifying them or replacing them with more efficient JOINs can improve both query readability and performance.

In addition to focusing on the query structure itself, optimizing database schema design is essential for improving overall performance. For instance, ensuring that foreign key relationships are properly indexed can dramatically speed up JOIN operations between related tables. Similarly, using normalization techniques to eliminate redundant data can help streamline queries by reducing the need for costly operations such as joins or aggregations over large datasets. However, in some cases, denormalization may be appropriate, especially when performance is critical. Denormalization involves intentionally introducing some redundancy into the schema to reduce the complexity of joins and enhance query performance. While this approach can improve read performance, it must be used carefully, as it can lead to issues with data consistency and maintenance.

Efficient use of joins is another key factor in optimizing SQL queries. In multi-table queries, understanding the type of join being used and the order in which tables are joined can have a significant impact on performance. For example, using INNER JOIN is generally more efficient than using OUTER JOINs because INNER JOINs only return rows with matching values in both tables, while OUTER JOINs return all rows from one table and NULLs for the unmatched rows in the other table. To further optimize joins, it is essential to ensure that the tables being joined are indexed on the columns used in the join condition. This allows the database engine to quickly match the rows and produce the result set without having to scan each table completely.

Query performance can also be influenced by the way the data is filtered and aggregated. Using WHERE clauses efficiently is crucial for limiting the amount of data processed in a query. Filtering rows early in the query reduces the number of rows the database has to deal with for subsequent operations, such as sorting or joining. When working with aggregate functions like COUNT, SUM, or AVG, ensuring that the aggregation is done after filtering the data can improve performance by limiting the data set to only relevant rows before performing the calculation. Additionally, using indexes on columns involved in filtering conditions can significantly improve the speed of queries that rely on these columns.

Database design and optimization often involve a trade-off between performance and maintainability. While optimizing for speed is important, the structure of the database must also remain flexible enough to support future growth and changes. Therefore, it is important to consider the long-term impact of optimizations on the system's scalability and ease of maintenance. For example, while denormalization may improve performance in the short term, it can complicate future changes to the database schema and increase the risk of data anomalies. On the other hand, adhering strictly to normalization principles can reduce redundancy and maintain data integrity but may require additional processing time for complex queries that involve many joins.

Another key consideration in optimizing SQL queries is the use of caching. Caching involves storing the results of frequently run queries in memory so that they can be quickly retrieved without having to execute the query again. By caching query results, databases can save time and resources, especially for read-heavy workloads. Caching mechanisms can be implemented at various levels, such as the application level, database level, or even the operating system level. However, caching must be managed carefully, as outdated or stale data in the cache can lead to inaccurate results. Therefore, it is important to implement cache invalidation strategies to ensure that cached data is refreshed appropriately when underlying data changes.

Finally, regular monitoring and performance tuning are essential for maintaining optimal query performance over time. Databases and query patterns evolve as data grows and business requirements change.

Therefore, it is crucial to periodically assess query performance, identify bottlenecks, and adjust database configurations, indexes, and query structures accordingly. Many modern database systems provide tools and utilities for profiling queries, analyzing execution plans, and identifying slow or inefficient queries. By regularly reviewing and optimizing the performance of the database and queries, administrators can ensure that the system continues to perform well as it scales and evolves.

Optimizing SQL queries for better performance is a multifaceted process that involves attention to detail in the design of both the queries and the database schema. Effective query optimization requires a deep understanding of the data, the types of queries being executed, and the database management system's query execution strategies. By focusing on query structure, indexing, join strategies, and caching, as well as maintaining a well-designed schema and monitoring performance, database administrators can ensure that SQL queries run efficiently and that the database can handle increasingly complex workloads without compromising performance.

Database Partitioning: Managing Large Data Sets

As databases grow larger and more complex, managing and retrieving data efficiently becomes increasingly difficult. In relational databases, one of the most effective strategies for managing large datasets is partitioning. Database partitioning is the process of dividing a large database into smaller, more manageable pieces, known as partitions, which can then be managed and accessed independently. Partitioning can be done in several ways, and the specific approach chosen depends on the nature of the data, the queries being executed, and the overall system architecture. By breaking a large dataset into smaller parts, partitioning improves query performance, simplifies data management, and ensures that the database can scale as the amount of data increases.

One of the main advantages of partitioning is the ability to manage and query large datasets more efficiently. As data grows, certain operations, such as full table scans or complex joins, can become slow and resource-intensive. With partitioning, the database can limit the scope of these operations to just the relevant partitions, reducing the amount of data that needs to be processed and improving query performance. For example, in a sales database, partitioning data by region or date could allow the database to search only within the relevant region or time period, rather than scanning the entire dataset. This can lead to significant improvements in performance, especially in cases where data retrieval or aggregation involves large amounts of data.

There are several methods of partitioning a database, each with its own use cases and benefits. The most common types of partitioning include horizontal partitioning, vertical partitioning, and functional partitioning. Horizontal partitioning, also known as data partitioning or sharding, involves dividing a table into smaller subsets of rows, where each subset is stored in a separate partition. For example, a customer table might be partitioned by region, with each region's customer data stored in a different partition. This allows the database to distribute the load across multiple storage devices, improving query performance and ensuring that the database can handle increasing data volumes. Horizontal partitioning is particularly useful in scenarios where queries tend to focus on specific subsets of data, such as in reporting applications where data for a particular time period or geographical region is requested frequently.

Vertical partitioning, on the other hand, involves dividing a table by columns, with each partition storing a subset of the columns rather than rows. For example, if a table contains customer information, such as name, address, and phone number, vertical partitioning might store the name and address in one partition and the phone number in another. This approach is often used when certain columns are frequently accessed together, while others are accessed less often. By isolating frequently queried columns into separate partitions, the database can improve access times for common queries and reduce the amount of data that needs to be read from storage. Vertical partitioning can also help optimize storage by placing less frequently accessed columns on slower storage devices, while more frequently accessed columns are stored on faster devices.

Functional partitioning is another technique that involves dividing data based on specific business functions or categories. This method is often used in scenarios where data can be logically divided by the business logic or operations that it supports. For example, in an e-commerce database, data related to customer orders could be stored in one partition, while inventory data could be stored in another. This allows for more efficient data management and enables the database to handle different types of queries more effectively. Functional partitioning is particularly useful when different types of data require different performance optimizations or when certain business operations need to be isolated from others.

One of the key considerations when implementing partitioning is how to manage data access across partitions. Partitioning can make data access more efficient, but it also introduces the challenge of ensuring that queries that span multiple partitions are handled correctly. In many cases, databases use partitioning keys or indexes to determine which partition to access for a particular query. For example, when a query requests data for a specific region, the database uses the partitioning key (such as the region field) to locate the relevant partition. If the query requires data from multiple partitions, the database engine can either execute the query on each partition individually or use a distributed query engine to combine the results from multiple partitions. This adds complexity to query execution, as the system needs to ensure that the right data is retrieved from the correct partition in an efficient manner.

Another challenge of partitioning is ensuring that data remains consistent across partitions. In some cases, a transaction may need to update data in multiple partitions, which can lead to issues with consistency and integrity. To address this, databases use techniques such as distributed transactions and two-phase commits to ensure that updates are applied consistently across partitions. These techniques ensure that either all partitions involved in a transaction are updated successfully, or the transaction is rolled back to maintain consistency. However, these mechanisms can introduce additional overhead, particularly in distributed database systems, where communication between partitions may require additional processing time.

Partitioning also introduces the need for effective data management and maintenance strategies. As partitions grow in size, they may need to be reorganized, rebalanced, or archived to ensure that the database remains efficient. For example, in a partitioned database, it may be necessary to periodically merge smaller partitions, split large partitions, or move partitions to different storage devices to maintain optimal performance. Additionally, partitioning can introduce challenges when it comes to backup and recovery. Since partitions are independent, backups must be carefully coordinated to ensure that all partitions are backed up consistently. Similarly, during recovery, the system needs to restore each partition and ensure that the data across all partitions is consistent.

One of the main benefits of partitioning is its ability to improve scalability. As data grows, the database can add more partitions to handle the increased load, allowing the system to scale horizontally. This is particularly important for large-scale applications that need to support increasing volumes of data without sacrificing performance. Partitioning also enables better distribution of data across multiple servers or storage devices, which can improve fault tolerance and ensure high availability. In a partitioned database, if one partition becomes unavailable due to hardware failure or maintenance, the rest of the system can continue to function without disruption. This makes partitioning an important tool for ensuring the reliability and resilience of large, distributed databases.

However, partitioning is not a one-size-fits-all solution. It is essential to carefully consider the structure and nature of the data when choosing a partitioning strategy. In some cases, partitioning may introduce more complexity than it solves, particularly for smaller databases or systems with relatively simple query patterns. In such cases, the overhead of managing partitions may outweigh the performance benefits. Therefore, partitioning should be considered a tool to be used when necessary, rather than a universal solution for all database performance issues.

Database partitioning is a powerful technique for managing large data sets and improving query performance in relational databases. By dividing a large database into smaller, more manageable partitions, partitioning helps to improve scalability, reduce query response times, and optimize resource usage. The choice of partitioning strategy—whether horizontal, vertical, or functional—depends on the structure of the data and the specific needs of the system. While partitioning can present challenges in terms of data access, consistency, and maintenance, when implemented correctly, it is a key tool in managing large, growing databases and ensuring their efficiency and reliability over time.

Relational Database Storage: Tables, Files, and Pages

In relational databases, the way data is stored, organized, and accessed is crucial to the system's performance and scalability. A relational database organizes data into tables, which are the fundamental building blocks of any database schema. However, understanding how tables translate into physical storage, such as files and pages, provides deeper insight into the internal workings of the database and its overall performance. At the lowest level, relational database storage is comprised of files and pages, which work together to store data efficiently. These underlying storage structures allow the database management system (DBMS) to retrieve, update, and manage data quickly and effectively, even as the database grows in size.

At the highest level, a table in a relational database consists of rows and columns, with each row representing a record and each column representing an attribute of that record. The structure of the table is defined by its schema, which specifies the data types and relationships between columns. However, tables are not directly stored in their logical format in memory or on disk. Instead, the DBMS uses a system of physical storage that organizes the data into files and divides those files into smaller, more manageable units known as pages. This organization allows the database to handle large amounts of data efficiently and ensures that queries can be executed quickly.

Files in a relational database represent the physical containers for storing the actual data. Each table in the database is typically stored in one or more files, depending on the database's design and the volume of data. These files are organized by the DBMS in such a way that they can be quickly accessed and managed during database operations. The database engine uses these files to write new data, read existing data, and manage updates and deletions. Files are also where indexes, metadata, and transaction logs are stored. Each file is often segmented into smaller units known as pages, and it is within these pages that the data is actually stored.

Pages are the fundamental units of storage in a relational database. A page is a fixed-size block of memory or disk storage that contains a set number of rows, depending on the row size and the page size defined by the DBMS. For example, a page might typically be 4KB, 8KB, or 16KB in size, though the exact size depends on the configuration of the database system. Each page contains a collection of rows from a table, and these rows are stored contiguously within the page. When data is inserted or updated, the DBMS writes the new data to pages, and when data is deleted, the corresponding rows are marked as deleted and may eventually be purged. Pages allow the database to manage large amounts of data more efficiently by breaking the data into smaller, fixed-size chunks, which can be loaded and manipulated independently.

One of the key benefits of using pages is that they allow for more efficient disk I/O operations. When a query is executed, the DBMS retrieves the relevant pages from the disk and loads them into memory for processing. This minimizes the number of disk accesses needed to retrieve data, as entire pages can be read into memory at once, reducing the overhead of fetching individual rows or blocks of data. Additionally, because pages are small and fixed in size, the DBMS can perform efficient buffer management, ensuring that the most frequently accessed pages are kept in memory, while less frequently accessed pages are swapped in and out of memory as needed. This approach to storage helps optimize performance, especially for large databases with complex queries.

The organization of tables into pages also has important implications for database performance, particularly when it comes to indexing. Indexes are typically stored in separate files, and they too are divided into pages. When an index is used to look up data, the DBMS reads the pages of the index file to find the location of the data in the corresponding table. The performance of index lookups depends on the structure of the index and the way it is stored in pages. For example, B-tree indexes are often used for efficient searching and retrieval, and they are structured in a way that minimizes the number of page accesses needed to locate the desired data. By organizing the index into pages, the DBMS ensures that index lookups are fast and require minimal disk I/O operations.

When data is updated in a relational database, the changes must be written to the appropriate pages. For example, when a row is updated, the old data is removed from the page, and the new data is written in its place. In some cases, the update may cause the row to exceed the available space in the current page, in which case the DBMS will move the row to a different page and update the page pointers accordingly. This process, known as page splitting, can lead to fragmentation over time, as rows are moved between pages to accommodate new data. Fragmentation can cause performance degradation, as more pages need to be read into memory to retrieve the same amount of data. Database maintenance tasks such as defragmentation or page compaction can help reduce fragmentation and maintain optimal performance.

In addition to managing data in pages, relational databases also use a system of page locking to ensure that concurrent transactions do not conflict with each other. When multiple transactions are accessing the same table or pages simultaneously, the DBMS uses locks to ensure that only one transaction can modify a given page at a time. This prevents issues such as data corruption, lost updates, or inconsistent reads, ensuring that transactions are executed atomically and consistently. The granularity of locking can vary, with the DBMS allowing locks to be applied at different levels, such as the row level, page level, or table level, depending on the specific needs of the transaction and the database.

The use of tables, files, and pages in relational database storage allows for efficient management of large datasets and enables the DBMS to handle complex queries with minimal overhead. By breaking data down into manageable pages and organizing it into files, the DBMS ensures that data retrieval, updates, and deletions can be performed quickly and efficiently. Additionally, the use of indexing, page locking, and buffer management helps optimize query performance and ensures the consistency and integrity of the data. As databases continue to grow and evolve, the ability to manage large datasets efficiently through the use of tables, files, and pages remains a fundamental aspect of relational database design. Understanding how data is physically stored and organized is crucial for database administrators and developers, as it provides insight into the inner workings of the system and allows for better performance tuning and optimization.

Backups and Restores: Safeguarding Database Integrity

In any database system, the integrity and availability of data are critical. As databases become increasingly central to business operations, safeguarding data through effective backup and restore strategies is essential for ensuring that the data remains safe from corruption, hardware failures, or human errors. A robust backup and restore strategy is crucial not only for disaster recovery but also for the protection of business continuity. Without effective backups, businesses risk data loss, which can lead to operational disruptions, financial losses, or reputational damage. Understanding the principles of backups and restores in relational databases is key to maintaining data integrity and ensuring that the system can recover from unexpected events.

At the heart of database backup strategies is the need for redundancy. Redundancy ensures that copies of data are stored in multiple locations, making it possible to recover from failures. Backups can be categorized into several types, with the most common being full backups, incremental backups, and differential backups. A full backup captures the entire database, including all tables, indexes, and associated data, and creates a snapshot of the database at a specific point in time. While full backups provide the most comprehensive protection, they can be time-consuming and resource-intensive, especially for large databases. As a result, full backups are typically performed on a periodic basis, such as weekly or monthly, while incremental and differential backups are used more frequently.

Incremental backups capture only the changes made to the database since the last backup, whether it was a full backup or another incremental backup. These backups are faster and consume less storage space compared to full backups because they only include modified data. However, they require more effort during the restore process, as each incremental backup must be applied sequentially to the last full backup in order to recreate the current state of the database. Differential backups, on the other hand, capture all changes made since the last full backup, making them larger than incremental backups but simpler to restore. Differential backups strike a balance between the efficiency of incremental backups and the ease of restoring data from full backups.

Database backups can be stored in different locations, including local storage, network storage, or cloud storage. Local storage typically involves backing up data to a dedicated disk drive or server, which can provide fast access and quick restores. However, local backups are vulnerable to physical damage, such as hard drive failures or fires. Network storage, on the other hand, involves backing up data to a network-attached storage (NAS) device or a dedicated backup server, providing greater scalability and the ability to store backups in a centralized location. Cloud storage has become an increasingly popular option for backups due to its flexibility, scalability, and the ability to store data offsite. Cloud backup services often provide automated backup solutions, ensuring that backups are performed regularly and stored in geographically distributed data centers, which helps mitigate the risk of data loss due to localized disasters.

In addition to traditional file-based backups, many modern databases offer transaction log backups. Transaction logs record all changes made to the database, including insertions, updates, and deletions, and they allow the database to be restored to a specific point in time. Transaction log backups are essential for point-in-time recovery, as they allow a database to be restored to its exact state as of a specific moment, even if a disaster occurs after the last full backup was taken. This capability is particularly valuable in systems that require minimal downtime or where data changes rapidly. By regularly backing up the transaction logs, database administrators can ensure that any changes made to the database after the last full or incremental backup are preserved and can be recovered in the event of a failure.

While backups are essential for data protection, the process of restoring data is equally important. A restore operation involves retrieving data from a backup and applying it to the database, often in the event of data corruption, hardware failure, or accidental deletion. The speed and efficiency of the restore process depend on the type of backup used, the backup strategy in place, and the overall size of the database. Restoring from a full backup is straightforward but can take longer for large databases. When incremental or differential backups are involved, the restore process can be more complex, as the database must first be restored from the last full backup, and then each subsequent incremental or differential backup must be applied in sequence.

To facilitate faster recovery times, many organizations implement database clustering or replication as part of their disaster recovery plans. In a clustered database environment, multiple database instances are configured to work together to ensure high availability. If one instance fails, another instance can take over seamlessly, reducing downtime and ensuring that the system remains operational. Database replication involves maintaining copies of the database on multiple servers, either synchronously or asynchronously, to ensure that data is continuously updated across all replicas. Replication can provide an additional layer of protection by allowing for quick failover in the event of a database failure, as well as supporting load balancing to improve performance during peak usage.

Testing the backup and restore process is an essential part of any backup strategy. A backup is only as good as its ability to restore the data when needed. Regularly testing backups through mock restore operations helps ensure that backups are valid, complete, and can be recovered in a timely manner. This process also helps identify any issues with the backup files, such as corruption or incomplete backups, before they become critical. Testing also allows database administrators to fine-tune the restore process, ensuring that it meets the organization's recovery time objectives (RTO) and recovery point objectives (RPO). The RTO defines the maximum acceptable downtime for the system, while the RPO specifies the maximum acceptable data loss in the event of a disaster.

Backup and restore strategies should also consider security and compliance requirements. Encrypting backup files ensures that sensitive data is protected, even if backup storage is compromised. Many industries have regulatory requirements that mandate specific data retention policies, backup frequencies, and recovery procedures, so it is essential to align the backup and restore process with these guidelines. Additionally, ensuring that backup data is properly stored and protected helps organizations avoid penalties and mitigate the risks associated with data breaches.

While database backups are essential for protecting against data loss, they also play a key role in ensuring business continuity and minimizing the impact of disasters. In addition to the technical aspects of backups and restores, organizations must develop comprehensive disaster recovery plans that incorporate not only the backup strategy but also the processes and resources needed to restore normal operations in the event of a failure. By regularly backing up data, testing restore processes, and implementing additional measures such as replication or clustering, organizations can safeguard their database integrity and ensure that data remains protected and available at all times.

Backups and restores are vital components of a database's data protection strategy. Effective backups ensure that a database can recover from failures and maintain its integrity, while the restore process ensures that the data can be recovered when needed. By implementing the right backup strategies, regularly testing the backup system, and considering the security and compliance aspects of backups, organizations can maintain high levels of data availability, minimize downtime, and ensure that their databases continue to function smoothly even in the face of unexpected events.

Database Monitoring: Why It's Essential

Database monitoring is an integral part of database management that ensures the smooth operation and optimal performance of relational databases. It involves the continuous observation of a database's health, performance, and resource utilization to detect potential issues before they become critical. In today's data-driven world, where databases support essential business operations, effective database monitoring is indispensable for maintaining high availability, preventing downtime, and improving overall system performance. Database monitoring provides the insights necessary to make informed decisions, optimize resource allocation, and ensure that data is accessible and secure.

As databases grow in size and complexity, they become more challenging to manage. The increasing volume of transactions, the growing number of users, and the constant flow of data require constant oversight. Without effective monitoring, issues like slow queries, resource bottlenecks, and data corruption can go unnoticed until they cause significant disruption. Database monitoring tools help database administrators (DBAs) track performance metrics, such as query execution time, disk I/O, CPU usage, memory usage, and transaction logs. These metrics provide an in-depth understanding of how the database is performing and highlight areas that need attention.

One of the primary reasons why database monitoring is crucial is that it helps detect performance degradation before it impacts end users. In a busy database, performance issues may not immediately become apparent to users, but they can gradually degrade the system's response times and efficiency. For example, slow-running queries may begin to consume more system resources, causing delays and affecting the experience of users. By monitoring query performance, a DBA can identify inefficient queries that need optimization, such as queries that involve unnecessary joins, unindexed columns, or suboptimal filtering conditions. Early detection of these issues allows for proactive tuning, such as query optimization, adding indexes, or restructuring data, all of which can restore performance to acceptable levels before users notice any significant slowdowns.

Another key benefit of database monitoring is resource optimization. As databases grow and evolve, resource allocation becomes increasingly important. A lack of monitoring can lead to over-provisioning or under-provisioning of critical resources such as CPU, memory, and storage. When resources are over-allocated, the system can waste valuable capacity, leading to inefficiencies and higher operating costs. Conversely, under-allocating resources can result in sluggish performance and system failures due to inadequate resources being available for database operations. Monitoring tools help DBAs track resource utilization patterns over time, allowing them to make data-driven decisions about scaling the database infrastructure, adjusting memory allocations, or adding hardware resources as needed. This ensures that the database runs optimally, with the right balance of resources to handle its workload.

Security is another critical aspect of database monitoring. Databases often store sensitive information, such as customer data, financial records, or intellectual property, making them a prime target for cyberattacks. Effective monitoring helps detect unusual activities that could indicate a security breach, such as unauthorized access attempts, changes to critical data, or irregular login patterns. For example, a sudden increase in failed login attempts might indicate a brute-force attack, while unauthorized modifications to data might suggest an internal security breach. Database monitoring tools often include features for tracking user activities, generating security alerts, and providing audit logs, all of which can be used to detect and prevent security threats. Regular monitoring ensures that any potential security risks are addressed quickly, helping to protect the database from unauthorized access, data loss, or theft.

Database monitoring also plays a crucial role in maintaining database availability and uptime. In high-availability environments, where databases are critical to business operations, minimizing downtime is paramount. Monitoring tools track the health of database instances and identify potential issues that might lead to service interruptions, such as hardware failures, network connectivity problems, or corruption of database files. By detecting these issues early, DBAs can take action to prevent downtime, whether by moving workloads to a standby server, repairing damaged files, or optimizing database configurations. Additionally, many monitoring systems offer features for setting up automated failover mechanisms, which automatically switch to a backup system if the primary system becomes unavailable. This ensures that the database remains accessible, even in the event of hardware or software failures.

Backup and recovery processes are another area where database monitoring is essential. Monitoring ensures that backup operations are completed successfully and on schedule. Regular backups are critical for data protection, as they allow for the restoration of the database in case of data loss or corruption. By monitoring backup jobs, DBAs can ensure that they are not only occurring regularly but also that the backups are valid and can be restored if necessary. Monitoring also helps to identify any issues with the backup process, such as failed backups, incomplete backups, or insufficient disk space for storing backup files. This ensures that the organization's data protection strategy remains effective and that data can be recovered quickly if needed.

Furthermore, monitoring tools help DBAs to track the health of database replication and synchronization processes. In distributed database systems, replication is used to maintain copies of the database across multiple servers or locations. Monitoring replication processes is critical to ensure that data is properly synchronized and that no inconsistencies or delays occur. For example, if a replica is falling behind the primary database, the DBA can investigate the cause of the lag and take corrective action. Effective monitoring ensures that replication processes are running smoothly, and it can alert DBAs to any issues that might impact data consistency or lead to data loss.

In addition to these technical benefits, database monitoring provides valuable insights into overall system trends. Over time, monitoring tools can track changes in database performance, query patterns, and resource utilization, providing a historical record of the system's behavior. This data can be used for capacity planning, identifying areas of improvement, and predicting future resource needs. Monitoring also helps with compliance and auditing, as the logs generated by monitoring tools can be used to demonstrate adherence to industry standards or regulatory requirements, such as data privacy laws or financial reporting standards.

Finally, database monitoring helps to optimize the performance of the entire database ecosystem, which includes not only the database itself but also the operating system, network, and hardware that support it. By monitoring the entire stack, DBAs can identify interdependencies between different components of the database infrastructure and troubleshoot issues that might not be immediately obvious. This holistic view of the system enables more effective troubleshooting, resource allocation, and performance tuning.

Database monitoring is an essential practice for ensuring the health, performance, and security of relational databases. By continuously observing key metrics and system behavior, monitoring tools provide DBAs with the information they need to identify and address issues proactively. From optimizing query performance to securing sensitive data and ensuring high availability, database monitoring is indispensable for maintaining the integrity of database systems and ensuring that they continue to meet the needs of modern businesses. Whether in the context of performance optimization, security management, or disaster recovery, monitoring is a critical aspect of effective database management.

Real-Time Database Monitoring Tools

In the world of relational databases, the need for real-time monitoring has become increasingly important as systems grow in complexity and scale. Real-time database monitoring tools are essential for providing immediate insights into the performance, health, and security of a database. These tools allow database administrators (DBAs) to monitor the database's activity and resource utilization in real time, helping to detect issues before they become critical and ensuring optimal performance. In environments where database downtime is not acceptable and performance is a key factor in business success, real-time monitoring tools provide a proactive approach to maintaining the health and integrity of the database.

Real-time database monitoring tools continuously track the database's performance metrics, such as query execution times, CPU usage, memory consumption, disk I/O, and network traffic. These metrics provide DBAs with critical information about how the database is functioning and highlight any potential bottlenecks or resource constraints that might affect performance. For example, if a database is experiencing high CPU usage or slow query execution, real-time monitoring tools can help pinpoint the source of the issue, such as a poorly optimized query, insufficient hardware resources, or a problem with indexing. The ability to observe performance in real time allows DBAs to quickly intervene and take corrective actions to restore optimal operation.

In addition to monitoring the database's internal performance, real-time monitoring tools also track database transactions, locking mechanisms, and query execution. Transaction monitoring is especially important for systems that support high transaction volumes or need to maintain data consistency across multiple users and applications. Real-time monitoring tools can detect long-running transactions, deadlocks, or locking contention issues that might cause delays or block other transactions. These issues can have a significant impact on database performance, as well as the user experience. By providing detailed insights into transaction activity, real-time monitoring tools help DBAs identify and resolve transactional problems before they escalate, ensuring that the database operates smoothly and efficiently.

Real-time database monitoring tools also play a critical role in detecting security threats and potential breaches. They can track user activity, authentication attempts, and data access patterns to identify unusual or unauthorized behavior. For example, if an unusually high number of failed login attempts are detected, the monitoring tool can alert the DBA to a potential brute-force attack. Similarly, if sensitive data is being accessed by an unauthorized user or if there are unexpected changes to critical database configurations, real-time monitoring tools can send alerts and trigger predefined security responses. These capabilities are essential for protecting the database from security risks, preventing data breaches, and ensuring compliance with data protection regulations.

One of the key benefits of real-time monitoring tools is the ability to analyze and track queries in real time. Query performance monitoring is particularly valuable in complex databases with large datasets, as poorly optimized queries can lead to significant performance degradation. Real-time monitoring tools can analyze queries as they are executed, capturing detailed information about execution times, the number of rows returned, and any indexes used. With this data, DBAs can identify slow or inefficient queries and take steps to optimize them, such as rewriting the query, adding indexes, or adjusting database configurations. This process of continuous query optimization helps maintain a responsive and efficient database, even as it grows and handles increasing amounts of data.

Moreover, real-time monitoring tools provide a comprehensive view of system resource utilization, which is crucial for ensuring that the database is operating within its capacity. By tracking CPU, memory, disk, and network usage in real time, these tools help DBAs detect potential resource shortages or imbalances that could lead to performance issues. For example, if disk space is running low or if there is excessive memory consumption, real-time monitoring can trigger an alert, allowing the DBA to take action before these issues cause a system outage or slow performance. This type of proactive monitoring ensures that the database operates within its optimal resource thresholds, preventing performance bottlenecks that could impact end-users or business operations.

Real-time monitoring tools also provide valuable insights into the health and availability of the database infrastructure. Many of these tools can monitor the database's underlying hardware, including servers, storage devices, and network components. By tracking the health of the infrastructure in real time, DBAs can quickly identify hardware failures, network issues, or storage problems that might impact the database's availability. For example, if a disk drive is approaching failure or if network latency is increasing, the real-time monitoring tool can alert the DBA to the issue, enabling them to take corrective actions, such as replacing faulty hardware or optimizing network configurations. This level of visibility into the infrastructure helps ensure high availability and minimizes the risk of downtime.

Real-time database monitoring tools also support scalability by helping DBAs manage the database's growth over time. As databases expand in size and handle more complex queries and transactions, real-time monitoring provides the insights needed to scale the database infrastructure effectively. By analyzing performance trends and resource utilization patterns, DBAs can make informed decisions about when to add additional hardware resources, distribute workloads across multiple servers, or partition the database to improve performance. Real-time monitoring tools can also provide capacity planning data, helping DBAs anticipate future resource needs and ensure that the database can handle increasing demand without compromising performance.

Another important feature of real-time monitoring tools is their ability to integrate with other database management tools, such as backup solutions, alerting systems, and performance tuning utilities. These integrations enable a seamless workflow for DBAs, allowing them to receive alerts, automate responses, and access detailed diagnostic information from a single interface. For instance, when a performance issue is detected, the monitoring tool can trigger an automatic backup to prevent data loss, or it can integrate with a tuning tool to recommend performance improvements. This level of integration enhances the efficiency of database management and allows DBAs to respond more quickly to any issues that arise.

In many cases, real-time monitoring tools offer reporting and visualization features that allow DBAs to create detailed dashboards, charts, and reports that present performance data in a clear and actionable format. These reports can be used to track long-term trends, identify recurring issues, and document changes in performance over time. By visualizing performance data, DBAs can gain a deeper understanding of the database's behavior and identify areas for improvement. This visual data representation also helps stakeholders and decision-makers understand the database's performance and resource utilization, providing them with the information needed to make informed decisions about future investments or optimizations.

Real-time database monitoring tools are indispensable for maintaining the performance, security, and availability of modern relational databases. By providing continuous monitoring of key performance metrics, transaction activity, resource utilization, and security threats, these tools help DBAs ensure that the database operates efficiently and effectively. They allow for proactive intervention, optimizing queries, addressing performance bottlenecks, detecting security breaches, and ensuring the database remains available and responsive. As databases continue to evolve and grow in complexity, real-time monitoring becomes an essential part of database management, helping organizations maintain smooth operations and minimize the risk of downtime or data loss. The insights gained from real-time monitoring tools empower DBAs to optimize the database environment, support scalability, and ensure the ongoing integrity of critical business data.

Database Performance Tuning: Techniques and Best Practices

Database performance tuning is an essential task in ensuring that a relational database system (RDBMS) operates efficiently and can handle increasing data loads without sacrificing speed or reliability. As databases grow in size and complexity, performance issues can arise, affecting the response time of queries, the system's resource utilization, and the overall user experience. Performance tuning involves identifying bottlenecks, optimizing queries, adjusting configurations, and implementing best practices to enhance the speed, scalability, and efficiency of the database system. A well-tuned database not only improves the overall performance of an application but also ensures that the system can scale effectively as the database grows over time.

One of the most effective ways to improve database performance is by optimizing SQL queries. SQL queries, especially complex ones, can often be the source of performance issues, especially when they are poorly written or inefficient. The first step in query optimization is ensuring that the database is using the appropriate indexes for search operations. Indexes allow the database engine to quickly locate the relevant rows based on a query's conditions, significantly reducing the time required to search through large tables. Without indexes, the database must perform a full table scan, which can be slow and resource-intensive. Proper indexing, however, requires thoughtful consideration. Over-indexing or poorly chosen indexes can introduce performance overhead, as the database must maintain these indexes during updates, inserts, and deletes.

Once appropriate indexes are in place, the next step in query optimization is to focus on the structure of the queries themselves. One common performance issue in SQL queries is the unnecessary use of SELECT * (selecting all columns). This can slow down performance, especially when dealing with large tables. By selecting only the necessary columns, the database retrieves and processes less data, improving query performance. Similarly, optimizing joins is a critical part of query optimization. Joins that involve large tables should be written carefully to avoid inefficient operations. For example, using INNER JOIN when appropriate instead of LEFT JOIN can reduce unnecessary data retrieval, and ensuring that join conditions are based on indexed columns can speed up the process.

Another critical aspect of performance tuning is optimizing the database schema itself. A well-designed schema can prevent many performance issues from arising in the first place. Normalization is a fundamental principle in database design that reduces redundancy and ensures data integrity. However, in certain situations, a fully normalized schema may lead to performance degradation due to the need for frequent joins across multiple tables. In these cases, denormalization—introducing controlled redundancy—may be an appropriate approach. By storing frequently accessed data in fewer tables, the database can reduce the need for joins and improve performance, particularly for read-heavy operations. However, denormalization comes with trade-offs, as it can lead to data inconsistency if not carefully managed.

In addition to schema design, tuning the database's configuration settings plays an important role in performance optimization. Configuration parameters such as memory allocation, buffer sizes, and cache settings can have a significant impact on how the database operates under different workloads. For example, increasing the buffer pool size can help the database store more data in memory, reducing disk I/O and speeding up query execution. Similarly, optimizing the database's transaction log settings can help improve write performance, ensuring that the database efficiently handles transactions without overburdening the system. It is crucial to carefully review and adjust these parameters based on the specific workload, hardware, and data access patterns of the application.

Monitoring and analyzing the database's performance is a key part of the tuning process. Regular monitoring helps identify performance bottlenecks and provides insights into the areas that require optimization. Tools that analyze execution plans are particularly useful in this regard. Execution plans show how the database engine processes a query, revealing whether it uses the appropriate indexes, performs unnecessary scans, or has inefficient joins. By examining execution plans, DBAs can identify areas where the query can be optimized, such as by adding indexes, rewriting queries, or adjusting database parameters. Regularly reviewing performance metrics such as query execution times, disk I/O, and CPU usage provides a comprehensive view of the database's health and allows DBAs to make informed decisions about optimization.

Another important factor in database performance is the management of transactions and concurrency. As more users and applications access the database concurrently, the likelihood of contention for resources increases. Transaction isolation levels define how concurrent transactions interact with each other, and adjusting these levels can help balance performance and data consistency. For example, using a lower isolation level such as READ COMMITTED instead of SERIALIZABLE can reduce locking and improve concurrency, but at the expense of potential issues such as non-repeatable reads or phantom reads. DBAs need to carefully assess the application's requirements for data consistency and choose the appropriate isolation level to avoid performance bottlenecks.

In addition to adjusting isolation levels, DBAs can use techniques such as connection pooling to improve database performance. Connection pooling allows multiple users or applications to share a limited number of database connections, reducing the overhead associated with establishing and closing database connections. By reusing existing connections, connection pooling improves response times and reduces the load on the database server, particularly in high-traffic environments.

Partitioning is another powerful technique for optimizing database performance, especially for large databases. Partitioning involves dividing large tables into smaller, more manageable pieces, known as partitions. Each partition can be stored separately, either on different disks or across different servers, improving performance by reducing the amount of data that needs to be processed for queries. Partitioning can be done based on various criteria, such as ranges of values, hash values, or time periods. By partitioning tables, the database can perform more efficient queries, especially when working with large datasets, by limiting the search to only the relevant partitions. This technique is particularly useful in environments where queries often filter data based on certain attributes, such as date or region.

Additionally, database performance can be improved by utilizing caching mechanisms. Caching frequently accessed data in memory reduces the need to query the database repeatedly for the same information, significantly improving response times. Many relational databases offer built-in caching features, but external caching systems such as Redis or Memcached can also be used to cache data at the application level. Caching is particularly useful for read-heavy applications, where certain queries or data are accessed frequently.

Finally, regular maintenance tasks, such as index rebuilding, statistics updates, and table optimization, help keep the database running smoothly. Over time, indexes can become fragmented, reducing their effectiveness and slowing down query performance. Rebuilding indexes periodically ensures that they remain efficient and help speed up data retrieval. Similarly, updating statistics about table contents enables the query optimizer to make better decisions about how to execute queries. Regular maintenance tasks help ensure that the database remains optimized as it grows and evolves.

Database performance tuning is a continuous process that requires ongoing attention, monitoring, and optimization. By focusing on query optimization, schema design, configuration tuning, and regular maintenance, DBAs can ensure that their relational databases operate efficiently and can handle the demands of modern applications. With the right techniques and best practices, a well-tuned database can deliver high performance, reliability, and scalability, supporting the growing needs of businesses and their users.

Database Security: Protecting Data and Access

In an increasingly interconnected world, the security of data stored in databases has become a critical concern for businesses and organizations. Relational databases store vast amounts of sensitive and valuable information, such as personal details, financial records, intellectual property, and much more. If this data is compromised, it can lead to severe consequences, including financial losses, legal repercussions, and irreparable damage to an organization's reputation. As such, database security plays a vital role in ensuring that this data remains protected from unauthorized access, tampering, and loss. Protecting data and controlling access are two of the most important aspects of database security, and they require a combination of robust technical measures, policies, and best practices.

One of the primary components of database security is protecting the data itself. This involves securing both the data stored within the database and the data transmitted between the database and other systems or users. Data at rest refers to the information stored in the database, while data in transit refers to data being transferred over networks. Both types of data require protection to ensure that they cannot be accessed, altered, or stolen by malicious actors.

Data encryption is one of the most effective methods for protecting data at rest and in transit. Encryption transforms readable data into an unreadable format using an algorithm and an encryption key. Even if an attacker gains access to the physical storage of the database, they will not be able to read or manipulate the encrypted data without the appropriate key. Many relational databases offer built-in encryption features, such as Transparent Data Encryption (TDE) for data at rest and SSL/TLS for encrypting data in transit. These encryption mechanisms help ensure that data is secure, even if the database is breached or intercepted during transmission.

In addition to encryption, database access control is a critical aspect of database security. Access control mechanisms help define who can access the database and what actions they can perform. These mechanisms ensure that only authorized users have access to the database, and that they can only perform the tasks necessary for their role. One of the most fundamental access control techniques is the use of authentication and authorization.

Authentication verifies the identity of a user or application attempting to access the database. The most common authentication methods include username and password, but more advanced techniques such as multi-factor authentication (MFA) and biometric authentication are also gaining popularity. MFA enhances security by requiring the user to provide two or more forms of verification, such as a password and a fingerprint scan or a one-time code sent to their mobile device. This significantly reduces the risk of unauthorized access due to compromised credentials.

Once a user has been authenticated, authorization determines what actions they are allowed to perform within the database. This is typically managed through user roles and permissions. Each user is assigned one or more roles that define their level of access, such as read-only, read-write, or administrator. By carefully managing roles and permissions, database administrators (DBAs) can limit access to sensitive data and ensure that users only have the privileges necessary to perform their job functions. For example, a finance employee may be granted access to financial records, while a customer support representative may only have access to basic customer information. This principle of least privilege reduces the attack surface by limiting the exposure of sensitive data.

To further strengthen database security, auditing and monitoring are essential. Audit logs record all activities within the database, including who accessed the data, when it was accessed, and what actions were performed. By regularly reviewing these logs, DBAs can identify suspicious activities, such as unauthorized access attempts or unusual changes to sensitive data. For example, if a user who typically accesses only customer data suddenly attempts to access payroll records, this would trigger an alert for further investigation. Monitoring tools can also track the performance and health of the database, ensuring that any abnormal behavior, such as sudden spikes in query volume or slow performance, is quickly addressed. Auditing and monitoring help ensure that any potential security threats are detected and mitigated in a timely manner.

Database security also involves securing the infrastructure that supports the database. This includes the operating system, network, and hardware on which the database runs. One important measure is securing the database server itself. This can be achieved by applying the latest patches and updates to the operating system and database software, as security vulnerabilities are often discovered in older versions of software. DBAs should also configure firewalls and intrusion detection systems (IDS) to protect the database from unauthorized external access. The network should be segmented to ensure that database servers are isolated from other systems and only accessible through secure channels.

In addition to securing the database infrastructure, protecting the database backups is equally important. Backups are essential for data recovery in case of hardware failures, accidental deletions, or malicious attacks such as ransomware. However, backups themselves can become a target for attackers if they are not properly protected. Encrypting backups ensures that even if they are stolen, the data remains unreadable. Additionally, storing backups in geographically separate locations, such as offsite storage or cloud services, can protect against physical disasters, such as fires or floods, that might affect the primary data center.

Another aspect of database security involves ensuring that sensitive data is masked or anonymized when appropriate. For example, in development and testing environments, it is common to work with copies of production data. However, using real production data can expose sensitive information to developers, testers, and other stakeholders who may not require access to it. Data masking or anonymization techniques alter sensitive data while maintaining its usability, so it can be used in non-production environments without exposing real user information. This is especially important when working with personally identifiable information (PII) or other regulated data types.

Regular security assessments and penetration testing are essential to identify vulnerabilities within the database and its associated infrastructure. These assessments help uncover weaknesses that might not be immediately apparent, such as misconfigured settings, outdated software, or vulnerabilities in the database schema. Penetration testing simulates attacks on the database to identify potential entry points for malicious actors. By conducting regular security reviews, organizations can ensure that their database security measures are up to date and effective in protecting against evolving threats.

Finally, it is important to consider regulatory compliance when implementing database security. Many industries are subject to strict data protection regulations, such as GDPR, HIPAA, or PCI DSS, which require organizations to implement specific security measures to protect sensitive data. Compliance with these regulations often involves implementing encryption, access controls, audit logging, and other security measures to ensure the confidentiality, integrity, and availability of data. Failure to comply with these regulations can result in significant financial penalties and reputational damage.

Database security is an ongoing process that requires careful planning, continuous monitoring, and the implementation of best practices. Protecting data and controlling access are fundamental components of any database security strategy, and they require a combination of encryption, access controls, authentication, monitoring, and infrastructure protection. By adopting a comprehensive approach to database security, organizations can ensure that their critical data remains safe from unauthorized access, tampering, and loss, while also maintaining compliance with industry standards and regulations.

User Authentication and Authorization in Relational Databases

In modern relational databases, the security of data is one of the most important considerations for ensuring that sensitive information is protected from unauthorized access. User authentication and authorization are fundamental concepts in this context, as they define who can access the database and what actions they are allowed to perform. Authentication is the process of verifying the identity of a user or system, while authorization refers to determining the permissions or access rights that a user has once their identity is confirmed. Both authentication and authorization work together to safeguard a database from unauthorized or malicious activity, while allowing legitimate users to perform necessary tasks. Proper implementation of these mechanisms is crucial for maintaining data security, integrity, and compliance with industry regulations.

The process of user authentication typically begins when a user attempts to access a database or application. The system requires the user to provide credentials, which are typically in the form of a username and a password. The username is used to identify the user, and the password is a secret key known only to the user. The database then compares the provided credentials against a stored record of valid users and their respective passwords. If the credentials match, the user is authenticated and granted access to the database. If the credentials do not match, access is denied.

While traditional username and password authentication is widely used, it is often considered insufficient by itself, particularly in environments where security is critical. Passwords can be compromised or guessed, and weak password policies can make systems vulnerable to brute-force attacks. To mitigate these risks, many organizations implement multi-factor authentication (MFA). MFA adds an additional layer of security by requiring the user to provide multiple forms of identification. For example, after entering a correct password, the user might be required to input a code sent to their mobile device or use biometric identification such as a fingerprint or facial recognition. By requiring more than one method of authentication, MFA significantly reduces the likelihood of unauthorized access, even if a password is compromised.

Once a user has been authenticated, the next step is determining what resources and actions they are allowed to access or perform. This is where authorization comes into play. Authorization defines the user's access level, determining which database objects they can read, modify, or delete, and what operations they can execute. In relational databases, authorization is typically managed through roles and permissions. A role is a set of privileges that can be granted to users, while permissions define the specific actions a user can perform on database objects such as tables, views, or stored procedures. For example, a user with the "read-only" role may only be allowed to query the database but cannot update or delete data, while a user with an "administrator" role may have full access to all database operations, including the ability to create or drop tables and grant permissions to other users.

To simplify management, users are often grouped into roles based on their job responsibilities. This role-based access control (RBAC) model allows administrators to define a set of permissions for a role and then assign that role to multiple users. By doing so, administrators can efficiently manage permissions without having to define individual permissions for each user. For example, a company might define roles such as "HR" for employees responsible for human resources tasks and "Sales" for those working in the sales department. Each role would have different levels of access to the database based on the needs of the department. The HR role might have access to employee data, while the Sales role might have access to customer data but not employee information.

Role-based access control helps prevent over-granting of permissions and ensures that users only have access to the data they need to perform their duties. The principle of least privilege is a key concept in this context, meaning that users should be given the minimum level of access necessary for their tasks. By adhering to this principle, organizations can minimize the risk of accidental or intentional misuse of data. For example, a salesperson does not need access to sensitive financial records, and a database administrator should not be able to modify customer data unless specifically authorized to do so. This principle is vital in reducing the attack surface of a database and minimizing the potential for data breaches.

In addition to roles, relational databases often use fine-grained access controls, which allow administrators to define more specific permissions on database objects. For instance, an administrator might grant a user access to a particular table but restrict access to specific columns within that table. This allows for a higher level of control over what data users can access. In some cases, database systems provide row-level security, where permissions can be applied to individual rows within a table. For example, a user might be allowed to view customer records only for customers in a specific region, while another user may have access to the entire customer database. Fine-grained access control enables organizations to enforce strict data access policies tailored to specific business requirements.

Another important aspect of user authentication and authorization is auditing and monitoring. Auditing refers to the process of tracking user activity within the database, including who accessed what data and what operations were performed. By maintaining detailed audit logs, organizations can ensure accountability and traceability for all database interactions. Auditing can also help detect unauthorized access or suspicious behavior, such as a user attempting to access data they are not authorized to view. Regularly reviewing these logs is an essential part of ensuring the integrity and security of the database. Monitoring user activity can help identify patterns of misuse, whether malicious or accidental, and enable proactive intervention.

To enhance security, it is important to regularly review and update user access rights. Over time, users may change roles or leave the organization, and their access privileges may need to be adjusted accordingly. User access reviews should be performed periodically to ensure that users no longer have access to data they no longer need. For example, if an employee changes departments or leaves the organization, their access to sensitive data should be revoked immediately to prevent potential security risks. By conducting regular access reviews, organizations can ensure that the principle of least privilege is maintained at all times.

In some environments, particularly those that deal with highly sensitive data or are subject to regulatory requirements, encryption plays a critical role in user authentication and authorization. Even if a user gains access to the database, encryption ensures that sensitive data remains unreadable without the proper decryption keys. This adds an additional layer of protection, ensuring that even if an attacker gains access to a database, the data itself is protected.

Authentication and authorization are integral to maintaining database security, ensuring that only authorized individuals can access sensitive data and perform critical actions. Through the use of strong authentication mechanisms, role-based access control, fine-grained permissions, and auditing, organizations can maintain control over who accesses their database and what actions they are allowed to perform. These security measures help to minimize the risk of unauthorized access, data breaches, and potential misuse, ensuring that the database remains secure and compliant with industry standards. In today's data-driven environment, effective user authentication and authorization are essential for maintaining the integrity and confidentiality of the information stored within relational databases.

Auditing and Compliance in Relational Database Management

In the world of relational database management, auditing and compliance are essential components of a well-rounded security strategy. As databases store sensitive and critical data, such as personal information, financial records, and intellectual property, it is crucial to ensure that access to this data is properly monitored and controlled. Auditing provides a detailed record of all database activities, offering insights into who accessed the data, what actions were taken, and when these actions occurred. Compliance, on the other hand, involves adhering to various regulatory frameworks and industry standards that govern how data should be stored, accessed, and protected. Together, auditing and compliance help maintain the integrity, security, and privacy of the data stored in relational databases, ensuring that organizations meet legal and regulatory requirements while also safeguarding against internal and external threats.

Auditing in the context of relational databases refers to the process of tracking and recording events or actions that occur within the database system. These events can include login attempts, data modifications, query executions, and administrative actions. Auditing is an essential tool for understanding who has access to the database and what operations they are performing. By generating comprehensive logs of user activity, auditing helps to ensure accountability, traceability, and transparency. In environments where databases handle sensitive or regulated data, auditing is particularly important as it provides an essential mechanism for detecting unauthorized access, tracking potential breaches, and investigating suspicious activities.

In a relational database, audit logs typically capture various pieces of information, such as the identity of the user performing the action, the specific operation being executed, the data affected, and the timestamp of the action. These logs can be configured to track a wide range of activities, from simple read operations to complex changes such as insertions, updates, and deletions. In many cases, audit logs also capture system-level events such as failed login attempts, privilege escalations, and attempts to bypass security controls. This detailed level of monitoring is critical for detecting abnormal behavior that might indicate a security threat, such as an insider threat or a potential external attack.

The role of auditing extends beyond just detecting security breaches. It is also vital for ensuring that the database is being used in compliance with organizational policies and external regulations. Many industries are governed by strict data privacy laws and regulations, such as the General Data Protection Regulation (GDPR), Health Insurance Portability and Accountability Act (HIPAA), or the Payment Card Industry Data Security Standard (PCI DSS). These regulations require organizations to track and control access to sensitive data, ensuring that it is used only for authorized purposes and is protected from unauthorized access or misuse. Auditing is an essential part of meeting these requirements, as it allows organizations to demonstrate that they are monitoring and controlling access to data in accordance with these regulations.

Compliance, however, goes beyond just auditing user activities. It involves ensuring that data is managed in a way that adheres to industry standards and legal requirements. For example, organizations must ensure that sensitive data is encrypted both at rest and in transit to prevent unauthorized access, even if the data is intercepted or stolen. Access controls and authentication mechanisms must be in place to ensure that only authorized users can access specific data sets, and that each user is granted only the minimum necessary privileges to perform their job. These controls are fundamental for protecting the confidentiality and integrity of data.

Many regulatory frameworks also require organizations to implement proper data retention policies. This means that data must be stored for a specified period before being securely deleted or anonymized. Failure to comply with data retention policies can lead to penalties and legal issues. Auditing plays a critical role here by tracking when data was created, accessed, modified, or deleted, making it easier for organizations to ensure they are complying with retention requirements. Moreover, organizations must maintain the ability to retrieve specific pieces of data quickly in the event of an audit or legal inquiry. Proper auditing mechanisms ensure that data can be traced back to its origin and provide a transparent record of its lifecycle.

For compliance purposes, relational databases also need to adhere to strict data access controls. This includes ensuring that only authorized personnel have access to sensitive data. Role-based access control (RBAC) is commonly used to enforce these restrictions, assigning users specific roles that determine their level of access to different parts of the database. For instance, an employee in a customer support role may have access to customer contact information but not to financial records, while an accountant may have access to financial data but not to customer support logs. By carefully managing access and regularly reviewing user permissions, organizations can prevent unauthorized data access and meet regulatory requirements for controlling sensitive data.

Auditing and compliance requirements often go hand in hand with disaster recovery planning. Organizations are required to have procedures in place to recover data in case of an emergency, such as a system failure, data corruption, or a cyberattack. Audit logs play a crucial role in this context as well, as they can help DBAs identify what data has been altered or compromised and provide a means of reconstructing lost or damaged data. Moreover, compliance regulations often require that organizations maintain secure backup systems and disaster recovery plans to ensure that data can be restored quickly and accurately in the event of an incident. Auditing helps to ensure that these systems are in place and functioning as required.

Additionally, modern database systems often include features that automatically enforce compliance rules and generate audit logs for critical activities. For example, relational databases may have built-in support for logging specific types of access, such as when users attempt to access sensitive fields like Social Security numbers, payment information, or medical records. These logs can be used not only for detecting potential breaches but also for demonstrating compliance with data privacy laws. Many organizations use third-party auditing and compliance tools that integrate with their database management system, providing a more centralized approach to tracking database activities and generating compliance reports.

One of the most significant challenges with auditing and compliance in relational databases is managing the vast amounts of data generated by audit logs. With high transaction volumes, the volume of audit logs can quickly become overwhelming, making it difficult for administrators to effectively monitor all activities. To address this, organizations often implement automated tools to analyze audit logs, identify patterns, and flag potential issues. Advanced techniques, such as machine learning and artificial intelligence, are increasingly being used to detect anomalies in real-time, reducing the burden on DBAs and ensuring that potential security threats or compliance issues are identified quickly.

While auditing and compliance practices are necessary for protecting data and ensuring regulatory adherence, they must be carefully balanced with performance considerations. Excessive auditing can add overhead to the system, especially in high-transaction environments. Therefore, organizations must fine-tune their auditing practices to capture the necessary information without overloading the database with excessive logging. For example, setting up filters to capture only specific types of activities or establishing retention policies for audit logs can help manage the volume of data and ensure the system runs efficiently.

Auditing and compliance in relational database management are not just about meeting regulatory requirements; they are essential practices for maintaining the security, integrity, and availability of data. By implementing effective auditing mechanisms, enforcing strict access controls, and adhering to industry regulations, organizations can ensure that they are managing their databases securely and in compliance with the law. Furthermore, audit logs provide valuable insights that help prevent security breaches, identify vulnerabilities, and facilitate recovery in the event of a disaster. In a world where data is one of the most valuable assets, ensuring proper auditing and compliance is a vital part of maintaining trust and protecting sensitive information.

Replication in Relational Databases: Benefits and Challenges

Replication in relational databases refers to the process of copying and maintaining database objects, such as tables and indexes, across multiple servers or locations. The goal of replication is to improve data availability, fault tolerance, and performance by ensuring that data is accessible from different servers in different geographical locations or across a distributed network. This mechanism plays a critical role in high-availability architectures, disaster recovery plans, and load-balancing strategies, making it an essential part of database management for modern enterprises. While replication offers several benefits, including increased reliability and scalability, it also presents its own set of challenges, particularly around consistency, latency, and resource management.

One of the primary benefits of database replication is enhanced data availability. In a replicated environment, data is stored in multiple locations, which means that even if one server goes down or becomes unavailable due to hardware failure, maintenance, or a network issue, other servers can continue to serve data. This redundancy is crucial for ensuring that users and applications can continue to access the database without disruption, even in the event of localized failures. For businesses that require continuous access to their data, such as e-commerce platforms or financial institutions, high availability is essential, and replication provides a reliable solution for meeting this need.

Replication also supports improved disaster recovery. By maintaining copies of data across different servers or geographical locations, organizations can quickly recover from data loss caused by natural disasters, cyberattacks, or human errors. For example, in the case of a data center failure or a catastrophic hardware malfunction, the database can be restored from one of the replicated servers. This makes it possible for organizations to minimize downtime and restore operations faster. Additionally, some replication setups allow for point-in-time recovery, where the database can be restored to a specific state at a particular moment, providing additional flexibility in disaster recovery scenarios.

Another significant benefit of replication is the ability to distribute database queries across multiple servers, thus improving performance and scalability. In a read-heavy workload, replication allows multiple copies of the database to be used for read operations, distributing the load and reducing the burden on any single server. This is particularly beneficial for applications that involve large volumes of read operations, such as reporting tools, data analytics, or online platforms with large user bases. By directing read queries to replica servers, the primary server is left to handle only write operations, improving the overall efficiency of the system. As the application grows and the database scales, replication enables the infrastructure to handle increased traffic without sacrificing performance.

Replication can also improve geographic distribution of data. For businesses with a global user base, having data replicated across multiple regions or data centers ensures that users experience low-latency access to the database, regardless of their location. This is particularly important for online services that need to provide fast response times to users in different time zones. By replicating data closer to the user, organizations can provide a more responsive and efficient user experience, while also ensuring that data is available even if one region experiences a failure or disruption.

However, while replication provides numerous benefits, it also introduces challenges that organizations must address. One of the most significant challenges of database replication is maintaining data consistency across replicas. In a replicated environment, there are often multiple copies of the same data, and ensuring that all copies remain synchronized is crucial. When data is updated on one replica, the changes must be propagated to all other replicas to maintain consistency. Depending on the type of replication used, this process can be either synchronous or asynchronous.

In synchronous replication, changes to the database are immediately reflected across all replicas, ensuring that all copies are always consistent. However, this approach can introduce latency, as every write operation must be confirmed by all replicas before the transaction is considered complete. This can slow down performance, particularly in geographically distributed systems where replicas are located in different data centers. Asynchronous replication, on the other hand, allows the database to write to the primary replica and then propagate the changes to other replicas in the background. While this reduces latency and improves performance, it introduces the risk of data inconsistency, as there may be a delay between when the data is updated on the primary replica and when the changes are reflected on the replicas.

Another challenge in replication is handling conflicts that may arise when multiple replicas are allowed to accept writes. In systems that use multi-master replication, where multiple servers can handle write operations, there is the potential for conflicting updates to the same piece of data. For example, if two users on different replicas update the same record simultaneously, the system must have a mechanism to detect and resolve the conflict. Conflict resolution strategies can include last-write-wins, where the most recent change is accepted, or more complex algorithms that involve user intervention or automated rules for resolving conflicts. Managing conflicts effectively is essential to ensuring the integrity of the data across all replicas.

Replication also introduces overhead in terms of resource management. Maintaining multiple copies of the database requires additional storage and computational resources. As the number of replicas increases, so does the cost of managing these copies, including ensuring that data is consistently synchronized and that backups are properly maintained. Replication can also increase the complexity of database administration, as DBAs must monitor the health of multiple replicas, manage failover procedures, and ensure that the replication process is functioning correctly. This adds to the administrative burden, particularly in large-scale systems with many replicas.

Monitoring and troubleshooting replicated databases can also be more complex than managing a single-instance database. With multiple replicas, it becomes more difficult to track performance issues, pinpoint bottlenecks, and diagnose failures. Issues such as lag in replication or network problems between replicas can cause discrepancies in data and lead to poor performance. To address these challenges, robust monitoring tools and alerting systems are essential. DBAs need to have visibility into the replication process, including tracking replication lag, monitoring system health, and identifying any issues that could impact data consistency or performance.

Finally, the choice of replication method—whether master-slave, master-master, or peer-to-peer—will affect how data is replicated and the complexity of managing the system. Each method has its own advantages and trade-offs. For example, master-slave replication is simpler to implement and more common in read-heavy applications, but it can introduce a single point of failure. Master-master replication offers greater fault tolerance and higher availability but requires careful conflict resolution and coordination. Peer-to-peer replication, while providing more flexibility, introduces greater complexity and is less commonly used.

Replication in relational databases is a powerful tool that offers many benefits, including improved data availability, enhanced performance, scalability, and disaster recovery. However, it also comes with its own set of challenges, including ensuring data consistency, managing conflicts, and addressing the additional resource and administrative overhead. Organizations must carefully consider these challenges when implementing a replication strategy and choose the appropriate replication model to meet their specific needs. By properly configuring and managing replication, businesses can take advantage of its benefits while minimizing the associated risks and complexities.

High Availability and Disaster Recovery in Databases

High availability and disaster recovery are two critical components of a comprehensive database management strategy. As businesses increasingly rely on databases to store and manage vital data, ensuring that these systems are always accessible and protected from disruptions is paramount. High availability refers to the ability of a system to remain operational and provide continuous service, minimizing downtime and disruptions. Disaster recovery, on the other hand, involves the processes, tools, and strategies used to restore a database to its normal state after a catastrophic event, such as hardware failure, data corruption, or natural disasters. Together, these strategies are designed to ensure that databases can withstand various types of failures while maintaining the integrity and accessibility of the data stored within them.

High availability in databases aims to reduce the impact of failures by ensuring that the system remains operational even when parts of the system fail. In a typical database environment, the database is managed by a single server, and any failure in this server can lead to significant downtime, potentially affecting business operations. High availability architectures, therefore, seek to eliminate or minimize this single point of failure. One common approach to achieving high availability is through database replication, where multiple copies of the database are maintained across different servers or data centers. In the event of a failure, the system can automatically redirect traffic to the backup copies, ensuring continuous access to the database. This approach can be implemented using various replication strategies, such as master-slave replication or multi-master replication, depending on the specific needs of the business.

Another method of achieving high availability is clustering, where multiple database servers are configured to work together as a single unit. Clustering allows for the distribution of workloads across several servers, ensuring that the system can handle high traffic volumes without compromising performance. In a clustered database environment, if one server fails, the remaining servers can continue to provide services, minimizing downtime. Clustering can be particularly useful for large-scale applications that require a high level of availability and scalability, such as e-commerce platforms or financial services.

Failover mechanisms are also essential for high availability. Failover refers to the automatic switching of database operations from a failed server to a standby server without user intervention. Failover systems can be implemented in both replication and clustering setups to provide seamless transitions in the event of a failure. When a failure is detected, the system automatically promotes the standby server to become the active server, ensuring that users continue to have access to the database without interruption. The failover process must be fast and reliable to prevent service disruptions, and it often requires careful configuration to ensure that data consistency is maintained throughout the transition.

While high availability strategies are designed to minimize downtime and ensure continuous access to data, disaster recovery focuses on the ability to restore data and services after a catastrophic event. Disaster recovery plans are essential for businesses that cannot afford to lose access to their databases for extended periods. A disaster recovery strategy typically includes data backups, failover systems, and procedures for restoring the database to a functional state after an outage. Backup strategies are a critical part of disaster recovery, and they can take several forms. Full backups capture the entire database, while incremental or differential backups capture only the changes made since the last backup. A well-designed backup strategy ensures that data can be recovered from a specific point in time, allowing for minimal data loss in the event of a disaster.

Data replication also plays a key role in disaster recovery by ensuring that backup copies of the database are available in geographically separate locations. In the event of a disaster that affects one data center, a replica stored in another location can be used to restore services. Replication also enables point-in-time recovery, where the database can be restored to a specific moment before the disaster occurred. This is particularly important for businesses that need to ensure that no data is lost during the recovery process. By keeping multiple copies of the database in different locations, organizations can reduce the risk of data loss and ensure that they can recover quickly from various types of disasters.

Testing and validation are essential components of disaster recovery planning. A disaster recovery plan is only effective if it can be executed quickly and reliably during an actual disaster. Regular testing of the disaster recovery process ensures that it will work as expected when needed. During these tests, organizations simulate different types of failures, such as server crashes or network outages, to ensure that the failover process works seamlessly and that the backup copies of the database can be restored quickly. These tests help identify potential weaknesses in the disaster recovery plan, allowing organizations to address any issues before they become critical.

In addition to replication and failover systems, cloud-based solutions have become an increasingly popular option for high availability and disaster recovery. Cloud providers offer services that automatically replicate data across multiple regions or availability zones, ensuring that databases are protected from local disasters. These cloud solutions provide flexibility, scalability, and cost-effectiveness, as organizations can scale their infrastructure up or down based on demand without having to invest in physical hardware. Furthermore, cloud services often include built-in disaster recovery options, such as automated backups and failover mechanisms, which help ensure that databases remain available even in the event of a failure.

While high availability and disaster recovery are crucial for ensuring that databases remain accessible and resilient, they also come with challenges. One challenge is the complexity of managing replicated databases or clustered environments. Configuring replication or clustering systems can be complex, particularly in large-scale environments where multiple servers and data centers are involved. Ensuring that all replicas are consistent and that failover mechanisms work reliably requires careful planning and constant monitoring. Additionally, managing the resources required for high availability systems, such as storage, network bandwidth, and processing power, can be resource-intensive, particularly as databases grow and demand increases.

Another challenge is the potential impact of high availability and disaster recovery systems on database performance. For example, while replication and failover systems improve availability, they can introduce latency and reduce the performance of write operations, as data must be propagated across multiple servers or locations. Similarly, backup processes can impact database performance, particularly if backups are performed during peak usage times. Balancing the need for high availability and disaster recovery with the need for optimal performance requires careful tuning and scheduling of replication, failover, and backup tasks.

Despite these challenges, high availability and disaster recovery are essential for businesses that rely on their databases for critical operations. By implementing strategies such as replication, clustering, failover systems, and cloud-based solutions, organizations can ensure that their databases remain accessible and resilient in the face of failures or disasters. Regular testing, monitoring, and optimization of these systems are crucial to maintaining their effectiveness and ensuring that they can quickly recover from disruptions, allowing businesses to continue operating with minimal downtime and data loss.

Cloud Databases: Relational Databases in the Cloud

Cloud computing has transformed the way businesses manage their IT infrastructure, providing a scalable, flexible, and cost-effective solution for data storage and processing. One of the significant advancements in this transformation is the rise of cloud databases, particularly relational databases hosted in the cloud. Relational databases have been a cornerstone of enterprise data management for decades, and their migration to cloud environments has brought about numerous benefits, including enhanced scalability, high availability, reduced infrastructure costs, and simplified management. However, transitioning relational databases to the cloud also comes with its set of challenges, such as data security concerns, performance considerations, and the complexity of migration.

Relational databases in the cloud refer to database services that follow the traditional relational model but are hosted and managed by cloud service providers rather than on-premises hardware. These cloud databases typically retain the core features of relational databases, such as tables, rows, columns, and relationships between data entities, while offering additional cloud-specific advantages. Cloud-based relational databases are designed to operate in cloud environments, taking advantage of features like distributed computing, on-demand provisioning, and elastic scalability. This enables businesses to scale their databases up or down based on demand, without having to worry about managing physical hardware or dealing with capacity planning.

One of the key benefits of using relational databases in the cloud is scalability. Traditional on-premises databases often require businesses to invest in large amounts of physical hardware, which can be costly and inefficient. In contrast, cloud databases provide the ability to scale dynamically. Cloud providers typically offer elastic storage and computing resources, allowing businesses to quickly increase or decrease their database capacity as needed. This is particularly useful for businesses that experience fluctuating workloads or rapid growth. For instance, during peak traffic periods, such as holiday seasons for e-commerce platforms, cloud databases can scale horizontally to accommodate the increased demand. When traffic subsides, the resources can be scaled back, saving on costs and ensuring efficient use of resources.

In addition to scalability, cloud databases provide significant benefits in terms of high availability. Cloud providers typically offer a range of features to ensure that databases remain accessible, even in the event of hardware failures or other disruptions. This includes automated backups, replication across multiple availability zones, and failover mechanisms. By replicating database instances in different geographic locations, cloud databases can offer redundancy, ensuring that if one region goes down, another can take over with minimal disruption. This level of availability is often difficult to achieve with traditional on-premises setups, which require significant investment in redundant infrastructure and disaster recovery systems.

Another advantage of cloud-based relational databases is the reduction in infrastructure management overhead. Managing an on-premises database requires ongoing maintenance, including hardware provisioning, software updates, security patches, and backups. These tasks can be time-consuming and resource-intensive, especially for organizations without dedicated database administrators. Cloud providers take on many of these responsibilities, offering fully managed database services that handle software updates, security, backup, and other administrative tasks. This allows businesses to focus on their core operations rather than managing the intricacies of database maintenance. Additionally, many cloud providers offer tools for monitoring and managing databases, providing real-time insights into performance, query execution times, and resource utilization.

Despite these advantages, there are several challenges associated with using relational databases in the cloud. One of the primary concerns is data security. Storing sensitive information in the cloud raises potential risks, as data is transmitted over the internet and stored on servers that are outside the organization's control. While cloud providers implement robust security measures, including encryption, firewalls, and access controls, businesses must still be proactive in ensuring that their data is secure. This includes configuring databases with appropriate access permissions, using encryption for data at rest and in transit, and implementing regular security audits. Additionally, businesses must ensure compliance with data protection regulations, such as GDPR or HIPAA, which govern how certain types of data should be handled.

Performance is another area that requires careful consideration when using cloud databases. While cloud platforms offer impressive scalability, performance can be impacted by several factors, including network latency, resource contention, and the configuration of database instances. In cloud environments, data is often distributed across multiple nodes, and requests must traverse the network to access data, which can introduce delays. For applications with high performance demands, businesses need to ensure that their database architecture is optimized for the cloud environment. This might involve configuring read replicas to distribute read traffic, optimizing indexes, or using caching mechanisms to reduce database load.

Migration is another challenge when moving relational databases to the cloud. Many businesses operate on legacy database systems that are tightly integrated into their on-premises infrastructure. Migrating these databases to the cloud requires careful planning, testing, and execution to ensure a smooth transition without data loss or extended downtime. Cloud providers often offer migration tools to help with this process, but it still requires expertise to handle issues such as data consistency, compatibility, and application integration. Additionally, businesses must consider how to manage data synchronization during the migration process to ensure that the cloud database remains up-to-date with the on-premises system.

Cost is another factor to consider when adopting relational databases in the cloud. While cloud services can offer significant cost savings compared to maintaining on-premises infrastructure, the pricing model can be complex. Costs are typically based on factors such as storage usage, compute capacity, and data transfer, which can fluctuate depending on the workload. Businesses need to carefully monitor their cloud database usage to avoid unexpected costs. Optimizing resource allocation, implementing auto-scaling policies, and choosing the appropriate instance types can help control costs. Cloud providers often offer pricing calculators and monitoring tools to assist businesses in estimating and managing expenses.

Cloud-based relational databases are typically provided as a service, with different cloud providers offering various models for database management. Some of the most widely used services include Amazon RDS (Relational Database Service), Google Cloud SQL, and Microsoft Azure SQL Database. These services allow businesses to choose from popular relational database management systems such as MySQL, PostgreSQL, Oracle, and SQL Server. Each cloud provider offers its own set of features, pricing models, and integration options, allowing businesses to select the best service based on their specific requirements. For example, Amazon RDS offers automatic backups, software patching, and scaling, while Azure SQL Database provides features such as elastic pools and serverless compute options. The choice of service depends on factors such as existing cloud infrastructure, specific database requirements, and performance needs.

In terms of integration, cloud relational databases can easily integrate with other cloud-based services, such as analytics tools, machine learning platforms, and data lakes. This allows businesses to leverage the power of the cloud to enhance their data processing capabilities and gain insights from their database. Cloud-native tools and services enable businesses to build more agile and responsive applications by integrating their databases with modern cloud technologies.

Relational databases in the cloud offer a wealth of benefits, including scalability, high availability, reduced infrastructure management, and integration with other cloud services. However, they also present challenges such as security, performance, migration, and cost management. By understanding these benefits and challenges, businesses can make informed decisions about adopting cloud-based relational databases. As cloud technology continues to evolve, the capabilities of relational databases in the cloud will likely expand, providing even greater opportunities for businesses to harness the power of their data.

Distributed Databases: Challenges and Solutions

Distributed databases have become an essential architecture for modern applications that require scalability, high availability, and fault tolerance. Unlike traditional relational databases, which are typically hosted on a single server, distributed databases spread data across multiple servers or locations, creating a network of interconnected systems that work together to provide seamless access to data. This architecture enables businesses to handle massive amounts of data, serve users across different geographical locations, and ensure that data remains available even in the face of hardware failures or network issues. However, while distributed databases offer significant benefits, they also come with a unique set of challenges that require careful management and innovative solutions.

One of the primary challenges of distributed databases is ensuring data consistency. In a distributed environment, data is stored across multiple nodes, and the system must ensure that all copies of the data are synchronized and consistent. Achieving this consistency can be difficult due to network latency, hardware failures, and concurrent access to the data by multiple users. The CAP theorem, which stands for Consistency, Availability, and Partition Tolerance, highlights the inherent trade-offs in distributed systems. According to the CAP theorem, it is impossible for a distributed database to simultaneously guarantee all three of these properties under all conditions. This means that in some situations, a distributed database may need to sacrifice consistency to maintain availability, or it may need to accept temporary inconsistencies to ensure the system remains available during network partitions.

To address the challenges of consistency, distributed databases often rely on different consistency models, such as strong consistency, eventual consistency, and tunable consistency. Strong consistency ensures that all nodes in the system have the same data at any given time, but this often comes at the cost of performance and availability. Eventual consistency, on the other hand, allows for temporary inconsistencies between nodes, but the system guarantees that, eventually, all nodes will converge to the same state. This model provides higher availability and performance but sacrifices consistency in the short term. Tunable consistency offers a middle ground, allowing the application to choose the level of consistency required based on the specific use case. For example, in some scenarios, it may be acceptable for a system to return slightly outdated data as long as it remains available. For critical operations, however, strong consistency may be necessary.

Another significant challenge in distributed databases is managing data partitioning. In a distributed system, data is often divided into smaller subsets, or partitions, which are distributed across different nodes. This partitioning enables the system to scale horizontally by adding more nodes as the database grows. However, partitioning introduces the complexity of determining how to split the data efficiently, and how to distribute and access data across multiple nodes. One common approach to partitioning is horizontal partitioning, or sharding, where rows of data are distributed across different nodes based on a partitioning key, such as a user ID or a timestamp. Sharding can improve performance by spreading the load across multiple nodes, but it also introduces challenges related to query complexity and data locality. When data is spread across many shards, queries that require data from multiple shards can become slower and more complex, requiring additional processing to combine results from different nodes.

Balancing the load across multiple nodes is another challenge associated with distributed databases. Ideally, each node in a distributed system should handle a roughly equal amount of work, but as data grows and traffic patterns change, some nodes may become overloaded while others are underutilized. This imbalance can lead to performance bottlenecks, slow queries, and inefficient resource utilization. Load balancing is essential to ensure that traffic is distributed evenly across nodes and that no single node becomes a bottleneck. Modern distributed database systems often include automated load balancing features that adjust the distribution of data and requests in real-time to ensure optimal performance. These systems monitor the workload on each node and automatically redistribute data or adjust routing mechanisms to prevent overloads and ensure efficient use of resources.

Network reliability and fault tolerance are additional challenges in distributed databases. Since data is stored across multiple nodes, the system must be able to handle network partitions, node failures, and other types of infrastructure issues without losing data or becoming unavailable. In traditional databases, if a server crashes, the database may become unavailable until it is restored from a backup or a failover mechanism is activated. In a distributed database, however, the system must be able to detect and recover from failures in real-time without affecting data availability. One common approach to achieving fault tolerance is replication, where copies of data are maintained on multiple nodes. In the event of a failure, the system can redirect traffic to another replica, ensuring that the data remains accessible. However, replication also introduces its own challenges, such as ensuring that data is consistently synchronized across replicas and managing the overhead of maintaining multiple copies of the data.

Another challenge in distributed databases is maintaining transactional integrity across multiple nodes. In a traditional, single-node relational database, transactions are managed using the ACID (Atomicity, Consistency, Isolation, Durability) properties, which ensure that database operations are reliable and consistent. However, in a distributed environment, maintaining these properties becomes more complex due to the need to coordinate transactions across multiple nodes, which may be geographically dispersed and experience network latency. Distributed databases often use techniques such as two-phase commit (2PC) or distributed consensus protocols like Paxos or Raft to ensure that transactions are consistently applied across all nodes. While these protocols help maintain transactional integrity, they can introduce latency and overhead, particularly in large-scale systems or systems with high network latency.

Security is also a critical concern in distributed databases. With data stored across multiple nodes, often in different locations, ensuring the security of the data becomes more complex. Distributed systems are more vulnerable to attacks, as each node in the system must be secured against unauthorized access. Additionally, the communication between nodes must be encrypted to protect data as it travels across potentially insecure networks. Managing access control and authentication in distributed databases is also more challenging, as the system must ensure that users have appropriate permissions across all nodes. A single compromised node could potentially jeopardize the entire system, making it crucial to implement strong security measures, such as encryption, firewalls, and multi-factor authentication, at each layer of the distributed database.

While distributed databases introduce several challenges, solutions have been developed to address these issues effectively. Modern distributed database systems, such as Apache Cassandra, Google Spanner, and Amazon DynamoDB, offer robust tools and architectures for handling data consistency, fault tolerance, and scalability. These systems often leverage advanced algorithms, such as quorum-based replication and distributed consensus, to ensure that data is consistent and available even in the face of failures. Additionally, advances in cloud computing have provided organizations with the flexibility to deploy distributed databases on-demand, with cloud providers offering built-in tools for replication, load balancing, and failover.

Distributed databases represent a powerful solution for managing large-scale data across multiple servers and locations. They provide significant benefits in terms of scalability, availability, and fault tolerance, but they also come with challenges related to consistency, performance, security, and complexity. As organizations continue to generate vast amounts of data and require faster, more resilient systems, the role of distributed databases will only continue to grow. By understanding the challenges and implementing the right solutions, businesses can take full advantage of the capabilities of distributed databases to support their data needs.

Database Scaling: Vertical and Horizontal Approaches

As businesses grow and their data needs expand, the capacity of their database systems often becomes a significant concern. Scaling a database is a critical challenge that organizations face in order to ensure that their systems can handle increasing volumes of data and traffic while maintaining performance and reliability. Database scaling involves adjusting the resources and architecture of a database system to accommodate growth, and it can be achieved through two primary approaches: vertical scaling and horizontal scaling. Both approaches have their advantages and challenges, and the decision on which to implement depends on the specific requirements of the business, the database workload, and the resources available.

Vertical scaling, also known as "scaling up," involves adding more power to an existing database server by upgrading its hardware components. This typically includes increasing the CPU power, adding more RAM, and expanding storage capacity. Vertical scaling is a straightforward approach to increasing the capacity of a database system, as it involves enhancing the performance of the existing infrastructure rather than introducing additional servers. By upgrading the hardware of a single server, businesses can improve the performance of their database, making it capable of handling higher loads and more intensive queries. This is particularly beneficial for applications that rely heavily on complex transactions or require significant processing power, such as data analytics platforms, enterprise resource planning systems, or customer relationship management tools.

One of the main advantages of vertical scaling is its simplicity. It is often easier to upgrade the hardware of an existing server than to reconfigure an entire distributed system. Additionally, vertical scaling allows for a more centralized system, where all data is stored in one place, making it easier to manage and maintain. There are no concerns about data distribution or network communication, as all queries are handled by a single server. Vertical scaling is also a good solution for applications that do not require high levels of redundancy or distributed resources, where increasing the power of a single server can sufficiently meet the growing demands.

However, vertical scaling also has its limitations. The primary constraint is that there is a physical limit to how much hardware can be added to a single server. At some point, the performance gains from adding more resources diminish, and further upgrades become either impractical or prohibitively expensive. For example, even the most powerful servers have finite limits in terms of CPU processing power, memory capacity, and storage throughput. As the database continues to grow and demand increases, vertical scaling may no longer be sufficient to meet the needs of the business. Additionally, vertical scaling does not offer redundancy. If the server fails, the entire database can go offline, leading to potential downtime and service interruptions.

Horizontal scaling, or "scaling out," offers an alternative solution by distributing the database load across multiple servers. Rather than upgrading a single server, horizontal scaling involves adding more servers to the system, which work together to handle the database traffic. This approach allows for the distribution of the database's workload, improving performance and capacity by utilizing multiple machines to process queries and store data. Horizontal scaling is particularly beneficial for systems that require high availability, as the additional servers provide redundancy in case of failures.

In horizontal scaling, databases are typically partitioned, or "sharded," across the multiple servers. This means that data is split into smaller chunks and distributed across different nodes. For example, a large customer database could be partitioned by geographic region, with each server handling a specific region's data. Each server is responsible for a subset of the data, and queries are directed to the appropriate server based on the data being requested. This partitioning allows the database to scale horizontally, as more servers can be added to accommodate additional data or higher traffic volumes.

Horizontal scaling offers several advantages over vertical scaling. One of the key benefits is its ability to scale indefinitely. As data or traffic grows, more servers can be added to the system, providing almost limitless scalability. This makes horizontal scaling ideal for applications that experience rapid growth or have unpredictable workloads, such as social media platforms, e-commerce websites, or cloud-based services. Horizontal scaling also offers redundancy and fault tolerance. If one server goes down, the other servers can continue to process requests, ensuring that the database remains available. This is crucial for applications that require high uptime and cannot afford to experience prolonged outages.

Despite its many benefits, horizontal scaling presents its own set of challenges. One of the primary challenges is the complexity of managing and maintaining a distributed system. Unlike vertical scaling, where the system is centralized on a single server, horizontal scaling requires coordination across multiple servers. This can involve complexities in data consistency, query routing, load balancing, and handling network latency. Ensuring that data is properly synchronized across all nodes is critical to maintaining consistency, and this often requires the use of replication and advanced algorithms for data synchronization. As the system grows, managing these distributed components becomes more difficult, and the risk of performance degradation or system failures increases.

Another challenge of horizontal scaling is the overhead associated with partitioning data. While partitioning helps distribute the load across multiple servers, it also introduces complexity in terms of data access. Queries that require data from multiple partitions may need to be processed by multiple servers, which can lead to increased latency and reduced performance. In some cases, cross-partition queries can be particularly challenging to optimize, especially in relational databases that rely heavily on joins or complex queries. Additionally, horizontal scaling requires careful planning of how data should be partitioned to ensure that the system remains efficient and easy to scale as the workload grows.

While both vertical and horizontal scaling have their respective advantages, many modern systems use a combination of both approaches, known as hybrid scaling. In a hybrid scaling model, vertical scaling is used to optimize individual servers within a distributed system, while horizontal scaling is used to expand the overall system. This approach allows businesses to take advantage of the strengths of both models, providing scalability and redundancy while also optimizing the performance of individual servers. For example, a cloud-based database might use vertical scaling to add more resources to its primary servers while horizontally scaling the system to accommodate additional traffic and data across multiple servers or regions.

The choice between vertical and horizontal scaling depends largely on the nature of the application, the workload, and the growth trajectory of the database. Vertical scaling is often simpler and more cost-effective for small to medium-sized applications or systems with relatively stable workloads. However, for large-scale applications or systems experiencing rapid growth, horizontal scaling provides a more flexible and scalable solution. By combining both approaches, businesses can ensure that their databases are prepared to handle increasing demands while maintaining performance, reliability, and cost efficiency.

Database scaling is a critical aspect of modern database management, ensuring that databases can handle increasing amounts of data and traffic without compromising performance. Vertical scaling offers a straightforward approach to boosting server capacity, while horizontal scaling provides an infinite level of scalability by distributing the workload across multiple servers. Each approach comes with its own set of benefits and challenges, and understanding how to effectively scale a database is key to ensuring that it remains responsive and resilient as the business grows.

Data Warehousing and Relational Databases

Data warehousing and relational databases are both integral components of modern data management systems, but they serve distinct purposes and are often used in complementary ways. A data warehouse is a system used to store and analyze large volumes of historical data, typically collected from multiple operational databases. It is designed to support decision-making processes by providing a centralized repository where data from various sources is integrated, cleaned, and stored for easy retrieval and analysis. Relational databases, on the other hand, are typically used for the day-to-day management of transactional data, supporting applications that require real-time access and updates. While both data warehousing and relational databases rely on similar underlying principles, their use cases, performance optimizations, and architectures differ in significant ways.

At the core of a relational database is the relational model, which organizes data into tables, with rows representing records and columns representing attributes. This structured format allows relational databases to efficiently store, retrieve, and manage data based on predefined relationships between tables. Relational databases support operations such as inserts, updates, and deletes, and they use Structured Query Language (SQL) to interact with the data. This makes relational databases well-suited for transactional systems that require quick responses to frequent read and write operations, such as customer-facing applications, online transaction processing (OLTP) systems, and inventory management systems.

A data warehouse, by contrast, is optimized for analytical querying and reporting rather than transactional processing. The data stored in a warehouse is typically historical in nature, and the focus is on providing a platform for decision support, business intelligence, and data analysis. Data warehousing systems store data in a denormalized format, often in multidimensional structures such as star schemas or snowflake schemas, which are designed to make it easier to perform complex queries across large datasets. In these schemas, data is typically organized into fact tables, which contain numerical data for analysis, and dimension tables, which contain descriptive attributes related to the facts, such as time, geography, or product categories.

One of the key differences between data warehousing and relational databases is the way data is loaded and updated. In relational databases, data is frequently updated in real time as users interact with applications. For example, a user may update their address in an online shopping platform, and the change will immediately be reflected in the corresponding table in the relational database. In a data warehouse, however, data is typically loaded in batches on a regular basis, often through an Extract, Transform, Load (ETL) process. During the ETL process, data is extracted from multiple source systems, transformed into a format suitable for analysis, and then loaded into the data warehouse. This batch loading process means that data in the warehouse is often not up-to-date in real-time, but rather reflects the state of the source systems at the time of the last batch update.

One of the reasons for this batch processing approach in data warehousing is the volume of data that needs to be managed. Unlike relational databases, which are optimized for handling small to medium-sized data transactions in real time, data warehouses are designed to manage vast amounts of historical data that can span years or even decades. This data often comes from a variety of sources, such as operational databases, external data feeds, and log files. Storing, integrating, and analyzing this data in real time would be inefficient and slow, which is why batch processing is used to load the data into the warehouse in a more controlled and optimized manner.

Another difference between data warehousing and relational databases is their focus on performance optimization. In a relational database, performance is typically optimized for quick reads and writes of transactional data. Indexing, query optimization, and caching are commonly used techniques to ensure that database operations are fast and efficient. Data in relational databases is highly normalized to minimize redundancy and ensure data integrity, which can sometimes result in slower query performance when multiple tables need to be joined for complex queries.

In a data warehouse, however, performance optimization is focused on enabling complex analytical queries across large datasets. To support this, data in the warehouse is often denormalized to reduce the need for complex joins, making it easier to retrieve the data required for business intelligence analysis. Denormalization involves duplicating data across tables to ensure that queries can be executed more efficiently, even if it results in some redundancy. Additionally, data warehouses often use specialized indexes, materialized views, and partitioning to further optimize query performance, particularly for analytical queries that scan large volumes of data.

Despite their differences, relational databases and data warehouses are often used together in modern data ecosystems. In many organizations, transactional data is first captured and stored in relational databases, where it can be accessed and updated in real time by users and applications. Over time, this data is then transferred to a data warehouse, where it can be analyzed and used for decision support. For example, an e-commerce platform may store customer orders, inventory levels, and shipping information in a relational database, while using a data warehouse to aggregate and analyze sales trends, customer behavior, and inventory forecasts.

The integration of relational databases and data warehouses is typically facilitated through the ETL process. Data from operational systems is extracted from the relational database, transformed into a format that aligns with the warehouse schema, and then loaded into the data warehouse for analysis. The data warehouse serves as a central repository for business intelligence tools, such as dashboards, reporting systems, and predictive analytics platforms, which provide insights into business performance and help drive decision-making.

In recent years, cloud-based data warehousing solutions have become increasingly popular, as they provide scalable, flexible, and cost-effective options for organizations to manage large datasets without the need to invest in on-premises infrastructure. Cloud data warehouses, such as Amazon Redshift, Google BigQuery, and Snowflake, allow organizations to store and analyze massive amounts of data with minimal upfront investment in hardware. These solutions also offer powerful tools for managing and optimizing data, making it easier for businesses to scale their data warehousing operations as their data needs grow. Many cloud data warehouses also integrate seamlessly with cloud-based relational databases, enabling businesses to build unified data ecosystems that combine transactional and analytical data in a single platform.

Data warehousing and relational databases are both essential components of modern data management. Relational databases provide the foundation for day-to-day transactional data processing, while data warehouses support complex analytical queries and business intelligence. Though these two systems differ in their architecture, use cases, and performance optimizations, they often work together to provide organizations with the tools needed to manage and analyze vast amounts of data. By integrating transactional and analytical data, businesses can gain valuable insights that drive decision-making and improve operational efficiency. As data volumes continue to grow, the need for effective data management solutions that combine relational databases and data warehousing will only increase.

Data Migration: Moving Data Across Different Databases

Data migration is a critical process in modern database management, involving the movement of data from one database to another. As organizations grow and evolve, their data needs may change, leading them to adopt new database systems, upgrade existing ones, or consolidate data from various sources. Whether it's moving data between relational databases, from on-premises systems to the cloud, or between different database platforms, the process of data migration can be complex, requiring careful planning, execution, and validation. The goal of data migration is to ensure that data is accurately transferred, preserved, and remains accessible in the new environment while minimizing disruption to business operations.

The need for data migration arises for a variety of reasons. As businesses adopt new technologies, they may decide to move to a more advanced database system that offers better scalability, security, or performance. For instance, an organization using legacy systems might migrate to a modern cloud-based database to take advantage of the scalability and cost benefits offered by cloud computing. Additionally, organizations often migrate data as part of database upgrades or consolidations, aiming to streamline their systems or consolidate multiple databases into a single, unified platform. Whether upgrading a database or moving to a new platform, data migration must be handled carefully to ensure data integrity, minimize downtime, and avoid data loss.

One of the first steps in data migration is data assessment. Before any actual migration can take place, the source database must be analyzed to understand the structure, dependencies, and relationships between the data. This includes identifying the types of data being stored, the relationships between tables or objects, and the specific requirements of the target database system. In some cases, the target system may require data to be formatted or transformed in a specific way to be compatible with the new environment. This process, known as data mapping, involves aligning data fields, types, and structures between the source and target systems. For example, a field storing a date in one format may need to be converted to another format to match the requirements of the destination database.

Once the data assessment and mapping are complete, the next step is the actual migration process. Data migration can be performed using a variety of methods, depending on the complexity of the migration, the size of the data, and the requirements of the business. One common method of data migration is through direct database transfers, where data is extracted from the source system and loaded into the target system using migration tools or scripts. This can be done either in real-time or through batch processing, depending on the business's tolerance for downtime. For small migrations, tools like database dumps or SQL scripts may be used to extract and import data manually. However, for large-scale migrations or those involving complex data transformations, dedicated migration tools or platforms are often employed to streamline the process and ensure data consistency.

Another important aspect of data migration is ensuring data quality during the transfer. Data quality refers to the accuracy, completeness, and consistency of data throughout the migration process. During migration, there is always a risk of data corruption, truncation, or loss. To mitigate these risks, it is crucial to implement rigorous testing and validation procedures both before and after the migration. Data validation checks should ensure that the data in the target system is complete, accurate, and correctly formatted. Additionally, it is important to ensure that all relationships and dependencies between data entities are preserved during migration, particularly in relational databases where foreign key constraints and other integrity rules must be maintained.

The migration process also needs to account for potential data transformation. This is especially important when moving data between different types of database systems, such as from a legacy relational database to a NoSQL database or from an on-premises system to a cloud platform. In these cases, the data may need to be transformed to fit the target system's requirements. For example, in relational databases, data is typically structured in tables with rows and columns, while NoSQL databases may store data in more flexible formats such as key-value pairs or documents. The migration process may require the restructuring of data to fit the schema of the target system, which can add complexity and require custom transformation logic.

As organizations increasingly move to the cloud, cloud-based data migration has become a significant focus. Migrating data to the cloud offers several advantages, such as improved scalability, cost efficiency, and accessibility. However, cloud migration presents unique challenges. One of the primary concerns is data security. When moving sensitive or regulated data to the cloud, businesses must ensure that the migration process complies with relevant data protection regulations, such as GDPR or HIPAA. This may involve using encryption during the transfer process and ensuring that the cloud service provider offers the necessary security controls and certifications to protect data in transit and at rest.

Cloud migrations often involve the use of specialized tools and services provided by cloud vendors. For example, Amazon Web Services (AWS), Microsoft Azure, and Google Cloud Platform all offer migration services to help businesses move data to their cloud environments. These tools are designed to simplify the migration process by automating many of the tasks involved, such as data extraction, transformation, and loading (ETL), and offering monitoring capabilities to track the progress of the migration. However, even with these tools, careful planning and testing are required to ensure a smooth transition and avoid disruptions to operations.

Another challenge in data migration is managing the potential impact on business continuity. Migrating large volumes of data, especially during working hours, can impact the performance of both the source and target systems, causing slowdowns or downtime. To minimize disruption, businesses often plan migrations during off-peak hours or perform the migration in phases. In some cases, hybrid approaches are used, where data is moved gradually over time to minimize the impact. During this process, businesses must also ensure that both systems remain synchronized, with real-time replication or interim databases to prevent data inconsistencies between the source and target systems.

After the migration process is complete, post-migration validation is essential to ensure that the data is properly integrated into the target system and that everything is functioning as expected. This phase involves testing the integrity of the data, checking system performance, and ensuring that all applications and users can access the data as needed. Additionally, businesses should have a rollback plan in place in case issues arise during the migration, allowing them to revert to the previous system if necessary.

The success of a data migration project relies heavily on careful planning, testing, and monitoring throughout the entire process. It is important for organizations to understand the complexities involved in moving data from one system to another, whether for cloud migration, platform upgrades, or data consolidation. By properly managing the migration, businesses can ensure that data remains secure, accurate, and accessible, allowing them to leverage their databases for enhanced decision-making and operational efficiency.

Data Modeling: Best Practices for Effective Database Design

Data modeling is a critical step in the design and creation of a relational database system, as it forms the foundation for how data is structured, stored, and accessed. An effective data model allows businesses to manage their data efficiently, ensuring that it is accurate, consistent, and easily retrievable. The process of data modeling involves defining the relationships between data entities, organizing data into tables, and ensuring that the design supports the functional and performance requirements of the database. A well-designed database is essential not only for efficient data storage but also for enabling robust data analysis and reporting. Data modeling requires careful planning and consideration of several best practices to ensure that the final design meets the organization's current and future needs.

One of the first principles in effective data modeling is to understand the business requirements thoroughly. Before designing any database schema, it is crucial to have a clear understanding of the data that will be managed and how it will be used. This includes gathering requirements from stakeholders, such as business analysts, application developers, and end users. By understanding the business processes and workflows, data modelers can ensure that the database design accurately reflects the needs of the organization. Additionally, understanding how data will be queried, updated, and reported on can help inform decisions about data structure, indexing, and optimization strategies.

Data normalization is one of the key techniques used in data modeling to eliminate redundancy and ensure data integrity. Normalization involves organizing the data into tables to minimize duplication and to establish clear relationships between different data entities. The goal of normalization is to reduce the chances of data anomalies, such as insertion, update, and deletion anomalies, which can lead to data inconsistency. The process typically involves dividing large tables into smaller, more manageable ones and defining relationships between them using keys. The most common forms of normalization are first normal form (1NF), second normal form (2NF), and third normal form (3NF), each of which addresses specific types of redundancy and dependency issues in the data structure. While normalization can significantly improve data integrity, it is important to strike a balance, as overly normalized designs can sometimes lead to performance issues due to the need for multiple joins.

However, in some cases, denormalization may be necessary for performance reasons. Denormalization is the process of intentionally introducing redundancy into the database schema to optimize query performance, particularly in read-heavy applications. In systems where quick retrieval of data is paramount—such as in reporting and analytics—denormalization can reduce the need for complex joins and improve the speed of data retrieval. While denormalization can improve performance, it must be used carefully, as it can introduce the risk of data anomalies and inconsistencies. A good data model should be flexible enough to allow for denormalization in specific areas without compromising the overall integrity of the database.

Another important aspect of data modeling is defining clear relationships between entities using keys. In a relational database, relationships are established using primary keys, foreign keys, and unique constraints. A primary key uniquely identifies each record in a table, ensuring that each row can be retrieved and referenced unambiguously. Foreign keys, on the other hand, define the relationships between tables by referencing the primary key of another table. These relationships can be one-to-one, one-to-many, or many-to-many, depending on how the data is structured and how entities interact with each other. Ensuring that relationships are properly defined and enforced is critical for maintaining data integrity and enabling accurate and efficient queries.

In addition to normalizing data and defining relationships, effective data modeling involves thinking ahead about the future scalability and flexibility of the database design. As businesses grow and evolve, their data needs will likely change, and the database must be able to accommodate this growth. To ensure that the database can scale with future demands, it is important to design a data model that is modular, flexible, and easy to extend. For example, designing tables with the ability to add new attributes or relationships without disrupting existing functionality is crucial for future-proofing the database. Furthermore, anticipating future reporting or analysis needs and incorporating those requirements into the initial design can help ensure that the database can easily adapt to new use cases as they arise.

Performance optimization is another critical consideration in data modeling. While normalization helps maintain data integrity, it can also lead to performance challenges when dealing with large datasets or complex queries. To address these challenges, data modelers must consider indexing strategies and query optimization techniques early in the design process. Indexes are used to speed up data retrieval by allowing the database engine to quickly locate the required records based on specific search criteria. However, indexes can introduce overhead in terms of storage and maintenance, especially when the data is frequently updated. It is important to carefully evaluate which columns should be indexed based on the most common queries and the expected workload.

Additionally, partitioning large tables into smaller, more manageable subsets, known as partitions, can help improve query performance by reducing the amount of data that needs to be scanned during query execution. Partitioning can be based on various criteria, such as date ranges or geographic regions, depending on the nature of the data. This technique is particularly useful for large-scale databases or systems that handle massive amounts of data, where querying the entire dataset would be inefficient.

Another key best practice in data modeling is to ensure that the design supports security and data privacy requirements. Data security should be integrated into the design from the outset, ensuring that sensitive data is stored in a way that prevents unauthorized access and maintains confidentiality. This includes implementing proper access controls, data encryption, and ensuring that data is stored in compliance with relevant regulations, such as GDPR or HIPAA. Furthermore, the design should allow for auditing and tracking of user activity, which can help identify potential security breaches or unauthorized access.

Collaboration and communication with other stakeholders are also essential throughout the data modeling process. Data modelers should work closely with application developers, business analysts, and end users to ensure that the database design aligns with the business requirements and technical constraints. This collaboration ensures that the database design is not only efficient and scalable but also meets the practical needs of the organization.

Data modeling is a vital process that lays the foundation for successful database design and implementation. By following best practices such as thorough requirements gathering, normalization, proper relationship definition, and performance optimization, organizations can build databases that are efficient, scalable, and capable of meeting their data needs. Thoughtful data modeling enables businesses to manage their data effectively, improve decision-making, and create systems that can adapt to changing requirements and growing data volumes. The success of a database system ultimately depends on the quality of its design, making data modeling an indispensable step in database management.

Database Views: Simplifying Complex Queries

In relational database management, the complexity of queries often increases as the data being queried becomes larger and more intricate. This complexity can make it difficult for developers and users to access the data they need in an efficient and understandable way. To address this issue, database views offer a powerful solution. A database view is essentially a virtual table that is defined by a query. It provides a way to simplify complex queries, abstracting the underlying data and presenting it in a manner that is easier to work with. Views help streamline the process of querying, improve data security, and enhance the maintainability of database systems, especially as the complexity of applications grows.

A view in a relational database is a saved SQL query that is treated as if it were a table. When a view is created, the database engine stores the query and allows users to interact with it just like any other table, even though the view itself does not store data. Instead, when the view is accessed, the database engine runs the underlying query and retrieves the data dynamically. This means that views are always up to date, reflecting the latest data in the underlying tables each time they are queried. The ability to create views allows database administrators and developers to encapsulate complex logic into reusable, manageable components, reducing the need for repetitive and complicated SQL statements.

One of the primary advantages of using views is the simplification of complex queries. Often, database systems contain data distributed across multiple tables with intricate relationships between them. When users need to retrieve information from these related tables, the queries can become highly complex, involving multiple joins, subqueries, and filtering conditions. Writing and maintaining these complex queries can be time-consuming and error-prone, especially as the database grows and the data becomes more complex. By creating a view that encapsulates the logic of these queries, users can access the data in a much simpler form, using a single SELECT statement that references the view rather than dealing with the complexity of multiple joins and conditions.

For example, consider a sales database with separate tables for customers, orders, and products. A user who needs to retrieve detailed sales information for a particular customer might need to write a complex query that joins all three tables, filters the results by the customer's ID, and calculates various aggregates like total sales or order quantities. Instead of writing this query repeatedly, a view can be created that encapsulates this logic. The user can then simply query the view to retrieve the necessary information without needing to understand or deal with the underlying complexity. This approach not only simplifies the user's tasks but also helps prevent mistakes in writing complex queries, as the logic is abstracted away in the view.

Another benefit of views is that they can provide a level of data security. In a typical database, access to tables is granted based on user roles and permissions. However, there may be situations where users should not have direct access to all the data in a table. For instance, a user may need to access sales data but should not be allowed to view sensitive customer information such as email addresses or phone numbers. In such cases, a view can be created that restricts the columns or rows of data the user can access. The user can then query the view, which provides a tailored subset of the data while keeping the full table hidden from them. By using views in this way, database administrators can enforce security policies without the need to modify the underlying tables or data access rules.

Views also enhance the maintainability of database systems. As applications evolve, the structure of the underlying data may change. For example, a new column may be added to a table, or a table relationship may be modified. If complex queries are written directly against the tables, these changes may require significant rewrites of queries across the application, leading to potential errors and inconsistency. By using views, however, the complex query logic is encapsulated in one place, and changes to the database schema can often be handled by updating the view rather than updating each individual query. This approach reduces the effort required to maintain queries and ensures that the application continues to work correctly, even when the underlying database schema is modified.

While views provide significant benefits, there are also considerations and limitations to be aware of when using them. One of the primary concerns is that views can sometimes impact performance. Since views are not materialized (meaning the data is not stored separately), every time a view is queried, the underlying query must be executed in real time. If the underlying query is complex or involves large datasets, querying a view can be slower than directly querying a table, especially when the view is used frequently. In some cases, using indexed views or materialized views can help mitigate this performance issue by precomputing and storing the results of the view. Materialized views, in particular, store the result of the query and only update it at specified intervals or when triggered, providing faster access to the data at the cost of having to manage the refresh process.

Another consideration is that not all types of queries are suitable for views. For example, views that include complex joins, aggregation, or filtering logic may not always be updatable, meaning that users cannot modify the data through the view itself. This is because the database engine may not be able to determine how to propagate changes made to the view back to the underlying tables. As a result, views that are intended for reporting or querying purposes should be designed with this limitation in mind, and users should be aware of when a view is not appropriate for performing insert, update, or delete operations.

Views can also add complexity to database design if they are overused or misused. While views are a powerful tool for simplifying queries and enhancing data security, relying too heavily on them can lead to a tangled web of dependencies and make the database harder to manage. It is important to ensure that views are used in a way that complements the database design and does not introduce unnecessary layers of abstraction. Overuse of views can also lead to performance issues if they are not optimized properly or if too many views are stacked on top of each other, creating complex execution plans that are difficult to debug and optimize.

Ultimately, views are a valuable tool for simplifying complex database queries, enhancing data security, and improving the maintainability of database systems. By abstracting complex logic into reusable components, views allow developers and end users to interact with the database more efficiently and with fewer errors. When designed and used appropriately, views provide a powerful way to streamline query development, protect sensitive data, and ensure that databases remain flexible and scalable as they grow. While there are performance and design considerations that must be taken into account, the benefits of views make them an essential feature of modern relational database management systems.

Materialized Views: Improving Query Performance

Materialized views are an essential feature of modern relational database management systems, designed to improve the performance of complex queries by storing the results of those queries. Unlike regular views, which dynamically generate their results each time they are queried, materialized views persist the query results as a physical table within the database. This approach offers significant performance benefits, particularly in scenarios where the same query is executed repeatedly, such as in reporting systems or data analytics applications. By precomputing and storing the results of complex or resource-intensive queries, materialized views reduce the need to reprocess large amounts of data each time the query is run, improving query response times and reducing the overall load on the database.

The primary advantage of materialized views lies in their ability to store precomputed query results. For instance, a complex query that involves multiple joins, aggregations, and filters may take a significant amount of time to execute, especially if it involves large datasets. Every time the query is executed, the database must scan the underlying tables, perform the necessary calculations, and return the result. This process can be resource-intensive, especially if the query is frequently requested by multiple users or applications. By creating a materialized view, the result of the query is computed once and stored, so subsequent queries can retrieve the data from the materialized view directly without needing to repeat the expensive computation. This leads to faster query performance and reduced processing times, especially in environments with high query volumes or complex analytical queries.

Materialized views can be particularly useful in data warehousing and business intelligence applications, where large volumes of data need to be aggregated and analyzed. For example, in a sales reporting system, a query might calculate the total sales for each product category over the past year, grouped by region. If this query is executed frequently, it would be inefficient to repeatedly compute the totals from the raw data. Instead, a materialized view can store the precomputed sales totals, allowing users to quickly retrieve the aggregated data without waiting for the system to process the entire dataset each time. This can significantly reduce the time required for generating reports and dashboards, providing end-users with faster access to critical business insights.

While materialized views provide significant performance improvements, they do come with certain trade-offs. The most notable drawback is the need to refresh the materialized view periodically to ensure that it reflects the most up-to-date data from the underlying tables. Since materialized views store static results, any changes made to the data in the underlying tables after the view was created will not be automatically reflected in the materialized view. As a result, the view must be refreshed either on a schedule or upon demand to maintain data consistency. Depending on the frequency of data updates and the complexity of the query, refreshing materialized views can be resource-intensive and may require careful management to balance query performance with the overhead of refreshing the views.

There are different strategies for refreshing materialized views, each with its own implications for performance and data consistency. The most common methods for refreshing materialized views include full refresh, incremental refresh, and on-demand refresh. A full refresh involves recomputing the entire materialized view from scratch, which can be time-consuming and resource-heavy, particularly for large datasets. Incremental refresh, on the other hand, only updates the parts of the materialized view that have changed since the last refresh, based on the changes in the underlying data. This approach is generally more efficient than a full refresh, but it requires the database to track changes to the underlying data and may be more complex to implement. On-demand refresh allows the materialized view to be updated manually or automatically based on specific triggers or user actions, providing more control over when the refresh occurs.

The choice of refresh strategy depends on the nature of the data, the frequency of updates, and the performance requirements of the system. For example, in a reporting environment where data changes infrequently, a full refresh might be acceptable, as the cost of recomputing the materialized view can be offset by the performance gains during query execution. In contrast, in a system with high data update rates, an incremental refresh may be more appropriate to minimize the performance impact of refreshing the materialized view. Additionally, some systems allow for the use of "real-time" materialized views, where the view is automatically updated as changes occur to the underlying data, though this can be more challenging to implement and manage.

Another consideration when using materialized views is storage. Since materialized views store query results as physical tables, they require additional storage space. The more complex the query and the larger the dataset, the more storage will be needed to maintain the materialized view. This additional storage requirement can become significant in environments with large datasets or many materialized views. Therefore, organizations need to balance the performance benefits of materialized views with the storage costs. In some cases, it may be more efficient to store only the most critical materialized views, while relying on other optimization techniques such as indexing or caching for less frequently accessed queries.

Materialized views are also subject to certain limitations, particularly when it comes to the types of queries that can be materialized. Some database systems may impose restrictions on the types of queries that can be used to create materialized views, especially if the query involves certain complex operations such as subqueries, joins, or aggregations. In addition, materialized views may not be well-suited for use cases where the data changes frequently, as the overhead of refreshing the view may outweigh the performance gains. For highly dynamic or real-time systems, other techniques, such as caching or real-time data processing, may be more appropriate.

Despite these limitations, materialized views are a valuable tool for optimizing query performance in a wide range of use cases. They can significantly improve the performance of complex analytical queries, reduce the load on the database server, and provide faster access to critical data. By precomputing and storing the results of expensive queries, materialized views allow organizations to meet the performance demands of their users and applications while minimizing the computational cost of querying large datasets.

The use of materialized views is particularly advantageous in data warehousing and business intelligence environments, where large volumes of historical data need to be aggregated and analyzed for reporting and decision-making. Materialized views allow these complex queries to be executed quickly, providing business users with real-time access to the insights they need without overloading the database or slowing down the system. By carefully managing the refresh strategy and storage requirements, organizations can fully leverage the power of materialized views to improve the performance of their database systems and ensure that data is readily available for analysis and reporting.

Materialized views provide an effective solution for improving query performance in relational databases, particularly in environments where complex queries are run frequently on large datasets. By precomputing and storing the results of these queries, materialized views reduce the processing load on the database and allow for faster data retrieval. While there are challenges associated with managing materialized views, such as the need for regular refreshing and additional storage requirements, the performance benefits they offer make them a valuable tool in optimizing database operations. Through thoughtful design and careful management, materialized views can play a crucial role in ensuring the efficiency and scalability of modern database systems.

Triggers: Automating Actions in Relational Databases

Triggers are a powerful feature in relational databases that enable the automatic execution of predefined actions based on specific events or changes in the database. These events can occur in response to data modifications such as insertions, updates, or deletions, or they can be activated by other database events, such as logins or system-level changes. The primary purpose of triggers is to automate tasks that would otherwise need to be manually executed, ensuring that these actions are performed consistently and without human intervention. Triggers help maintain data integrity, enforce business rules, and optimize system performance by automating routine tasks such as auditing, validation, and cascading updates.

The concept of triggers is built around the idea of event-driven programming. A trigger is defined to monitor a particular event on a table or view, and when the specified event occurs, the trigger automatically executes a predefined action, which is typically a SQL statement or a series of SQL statements. For instance, a trigger can be used to automatically update an audit log whenever a row in a critical table is modified, ensuring that any changes are recorded for future reference without the need for manual tracking. This automation reduces the chances of human error and ensures that the appropriate actions are taken whenever specific conditions are met.

Triggers can be classified into several types based on when they are executed relative to the event that activates them. The most common types are before triggers, after triggers, and instead of triggers. A before trigger is executed before the database operation, such as an insert, update, or delete, is performed. This type of trigger is useful for validating data or modifying the data before it is committed to the table. For example, a before insert trigger can check whether the data being inserted meets certain conditions, such as ensuring that a new customer's email address is unique before adding it to the customer table. After triggers, on the other hand, are executed after the database operation has been completed. These triggers are often used for actions that need to occur after data is modified, such as updating related tables, sending notifications, or logging changes. Finally, instead of triggers replace the usual operation with the actions defined in the trigger. For example, an instead of delete trigger can be used to prevent deletion of records from a table and instead log the attempt or move the record to an archive table.

One of the most important use cases for triggers is maintaining data integrity. Triggers can be used to enforce rules that ensure data consistency across different parts of a database. For instance, a trigger can be set up to automatically update related tables when a record is changed. This is particularly useful for cascading updates, where changes to one record need to be reflected in other records. For example, when a customer's address is updated, a trigger can ensure that the corresponding address records in related tables are also updated automatically, preventing data discrepancies. Triggers can also be used to enforce constraints beyond what is possible with standard relational integrity constraints, such as automatically calculating derived values or checking that certain business rules are followed before data is modified.

Triggers are also widely used in auditing and logging changes to data. In many business environments, especially in regulated industries, tracking data modifications is critical for compliance and accountability. By using triggers, organizations can automatically log changes to important tables, such as who made the change, what was changed, and when the change occurred. This can help ensure that the database maintains a complete and accurate history of modifications, making it easier to monitor activity and investigate issues when they arise. For example, a trigger might automatically create an entry in an audit table every time a record in a customer account table is updated, storing the old and new values as well as the identity of the user who made the change.

Triggers can also be used for enforcing business rules. In many cases, a trigger is an effective way to ensure that complex business logic is applied consistently across the database. For example, a trigger can prevent certain actions from being performed based on business conditions, such as disallowing the insertion of records that do not meet certain validation criteria. A trigger can also be used to automatically calculate values based on other fields in the same table. For instance, if an order is placed in an e-commerce database, a trigger can calculate the total price based on the items in the order and update the order total field automatically. This ensures that the business rules are applied consistently and accurately without requiring manual intervention.

Another important application of triggers is in the management of cascading actions between tables. In relational databases, relationships between tables are often established through foreign keys, and cascading actions can be defined to automatically handle updates or deletions in related tables. For example, when a record in a parent table is deleted, a trigger can be used to automatically delete related records in child tables, preventing orphaned data from being left behind. Similarly, when a record is updated, a trigger can propagate that change to related records to ensure data consistency. This type of cascading behavior helps to ensure that the database remains in a consistent state, even as data is modified.

While triggers provide significant benefits, they also come with certain challenges. One potential issue is performance. Because triggers automatically execute actions whenever their associated events occur, they can add overhead to the system, particularly when the operations being triggered are complex or involve large datasets. For example, a trigger that performs multiple updates or queries can slow down the overall performance of the system, especially if it is triggered frequently. To mitigate performance issues, it is important to ensure that triggers are designed efficiently and are only used for essential tasks that cannot be easily handled by other methods.

Another challenge with triggers is the potential for unintended consequences. Triggers operate automatically, which means that they can sometimes cause unexpected side effects if they are not carefully designed and tested. For instance, a trigger that performs a cascading update might inadvertently cause a chain reaction of updates across many tables, leading to performance degradation or data integrity issues. Additionally, because triggers are often executed in the background, they can be difficult to debug and monitor. Without proper logging and error handling, it may be challenging to track down the cause of issues that arise from trigger execution.

Triggers also require careful management to avoid conflicts between triggers or with other database operations. For example, if two triggers are defined to respond to the same event in conflicting ways, it can lead to inconsistent results or database errors. To avoid such issues, it is important to clearly define the behavior of triggers and ensure that they do not interfere with each other or with other parts of the system.

Despite these challenges, triggers are an indispensable tool for automating database operations, ensuring data integrity, and enforcing business rules. They provide a means of handling complex tasks that would otherwise require manual intervention, making it easier to maintain consistent, accurate data across the system. When used correctly, triggers can significantly improve the efficiency of database operations, streamline workflows, and enhance the overall performance of relational database systems. However, their potential impact on performance and system complexity means that careful planning and testing are essential for ensuring their successful implementation. By understanding the strengths and limitations of triggers, organizations can leverage them effectively to automate key actions and maintain a well-functioning database environment.

Stored Procedures: Enhancing Database Logic

Stored procedures are a fundamental feature in relational databases, designed to encapsulate complex logic and operations in a reusable and efficient manner. They are precompiled SQL statements or sets of statements that are stored in the database and can be executed by calling the procedure with a specific set of parameters. Stored procedures allow developers and database administrators to encapsulate business logic, streamline data processing, and improve the maintainability of the database system. By shifting much of the logic from client applications to the database itself, stored procedures help reduce network traffic, ensure consistency, and enhance performance. They are particularly useful for tasks that need to be executed repeatedly or involve complex operations, such as data manipulation, validation, and aggregation.

One of the primary benefits of stored procedures is that they allow for the centralization of logic within the database. In traditional database management systems, applications typically handle much of the data processing, which means that logic may be repeated across multiple parts of the application or across various applications. With stored procedures, however, developers can encapsulate this logic within the database itself. This centralization improves consistency, as the same logic is applied to all interactions with the database, regardless of which application or user is accessing it. For example, a stored procedure that validates customer data can be called by various applications, ensuring that the validation is always performed consistently.

Stored procedures also help improve performance by reducing the amount of data that needs to be transferred between the client and the database. In many cases, client applications send SQL queries to the database to retrieve or modify data. If the application requires complex processing or aggregation of data, this can result in multiple round-trip communications between the client and the database, which can be slow and resource-intensive. Stored procedures allow for the encapsulation of complex logic within the database itself, enabling the database to perform the necessary operations and return the result in a single call. This reduces the amount of data transferred over the network and can result in faster execution times, especially for operations that need to be executed repeatedly.

Another advantage of stored procedures is that they enhance security and control over database access. By defining stored procedures, database administrators can grant users access to specific functionality without exposing the underlying tables or data structures. This helps enforce the principle of least privilege, ensuring that users can only execute predefined operations and cannot directly access or modify sensitive data. For example, a stored procedure can be created to allow users to update their profile information, but it can be designed in such a way that users are not able to directly update sensitive fields such as their password or email address. By using stored procedures, organizations can minimize the risk of unauthorized access or accidental data corruption, as users are restricted to predefined actions that are managed by the database.

In addition to improving security, stored procedures also enhance the maintainability of database applications. As business logic becomes more complex, the code required to support various database operations can become difficult to manage. By encapsulating this logic within stored procedures, developers can create modular, reusable components that can be easily updated and maintained. If a business rule or calculation changes, for example, the stored procedure can be modified once, and the change will automatically be reflected across all applications that rely on that procedure. This reduces the need for manual updates in multiple places within the application code and helps ensure that the logic is applied consistently across all use cases.

Stored procedures are also useful for performing batch operations and handling large datasets. In many database systems, operations involving large volumes of data can be slow and inefficient if not properly optimized. Stored procedures can be used to batch process data, executing complex operations in the database itself rather than relying on external applications. For example, a stored procedure can be designed to update the status of multiple orders in an e-commerce system, or to delete records that are older than a certain threshold. By processing these operations within the database, the workload is shifted from the client application to the database engine, which is optimized for handling large volumes of data.

In some cases, stored procedures can also improve transaction management and error handling. A stored procedure can be written to include logic for handling errors, rolling back transactions, and ensuring that operations are completed atomically. For example, if a stored procedure performs multiple updates to different tables, it can ensure that all changes are committed together, or, if an error occurs, it can automatically roll back the transaction to prevent inconsistent data. This type of error handling ensures that the database remains in a consistent state, even if an operation fails midway through execution.

Despite the many advantages of stored procedures, there are also some considerations and potential drawbacks. One of the main challenges of using stored procedures is that they can introduce vendor lock-in. Stored procedures are often written in proprietary SQL dialects that vary from one database management system (DBMS) to another. This means that stored procedures written for one DBMS may not be easily portable to another, making it difficult for organizations to switch database vendors or migrate to a new platform. This can create challenges for organizations that wish to maintain flexibility or use multiple database platforms, as they may need to rewrite stored procedures or develop new solutions to maintain compatibility across systems.

Another issue with stored procedures is that they can become difficult to manage and maintain as the database grows. Since stored procedures are often written in a procedural language, they can become complex and hard to debug, especially if they involve a large number of operations or intricate business logic. This can make troubleshooting and optimizing stored procedures more challenging, particularly if they are not well-documented or if they are used by multiple applications. Developers must take care to ensure that stored procedures are properly structured, well-documented, and optimized for performance, to avoid creating a maintenance burden down the line.

Furthermore, stored procedures can also pose a challenge in terms of scalability. While stored procedures are typically faster than executing individual SQL queries, they can still become a bottleneck if they are not optimized properly. As the volume of data increases or as the number of users executing the stored procedure grows, performance may degrade if the procedure is not designed to handle such workloads efficiently. In some cases, additional optimization techniques, such as indexing, query optimization, and partitioning, may be necessary to ensure that stored procedures continue to perform well at scale.

Stored procedures are a valuable tool for enhancing the logic and functionality of relational databases. By encapsulating complex operations, improving performance, and providing security and maintainability benefits, they offer a powerful way to automate tasks and streamline database interactions. When used effectively, stored procedures can help businesses improve the efficiency and consistency of their database systems while reducing the complexity of their application code. However, they must be carefully designed, optimized, and maintained to avoid potential drawbacks such as performance bottlenecks, vendor lock-in, and scalability issues. By leveraging the strengths of stored procedures and addressing these challenges, organizations can build robust, efficient, and scalable database systems.

Functions and Their Use in Database Design

In relational databases, functions are an essential tool for extending the capabilities of SQL and enhancing the flexibility of database design. Functions allow for the encapsulation of reusable logic that can be executed within queries, triggers, or stored procedures. Unlike stored procedures, which are typically used to perform operations that do not return values, functions are specifically designed to return a result. This feature makes them particularly useful for tasks such as data transformation, aggregation, and complex calculations. Functions play a significant role in simplifying database design, improving performance, and ensuring that the logic embedded in the database is both modular and maintainable.

Functions in database design serve a variety of purposes, and their utility extends across different aspects of database development. One of the primary uses of functions is to encapsulate frequently used logic that needs to be applied consistently across multiple queries or procedures. This can include common operations such as string manipulation, mathematical calculations, date formatting, or data validation. By using functions to encapsulate this logic, developers can ensure that the same calculation or operation is applied uniformly throughout the application, avoiding the need to repeat code and reducing the likelihood of errors.

For example, consider a database that stores employee information, including their hire dates. If there is a need to calculate the tenure of each employee, this logic might be used in multiple queries across different parts of the application. Instead of repeating the calculation in every query, a function can be created to calculate the employee's tenure based on their hire date and the current date. This function can then be called within any query that requires the calculation, ensuring that the logic is consistent and easy to maintain. Furthermore, if the logic needs to be updated or modified, it can be done in one place—the function—without having to rewrite multiple queries.

Functions are also invaluable in data transformation tasks. Often, data stored in a relational database is not in the desired format for presentation or reporting purposes. For example, numeric values may need to be converted to strings, or dates may need to be formatted according to a specific standard. Functions can handle these transformations efficiently, allowing for the dynamic modification of data as it is retrieved from the database. A function that converts a date from one format to another, or one that formats a phone number according to a particular style, can be used directly in queries or views, ensuring that data is returned in the correct format without the need for complex application-level logic.

In addition to simplifying query logic, functions also enhance the performance of a database by reducing the complexity of the operations being performed. Complex operations that would otherwise require multiple steps or intermediate results can be encapsulated in a single function call, making the overall query more efficient. For instance, a function that performs a series of aggregations or calculations can be called within a query to process the data in a streamlined manner, reducing the need for multiple joins or subqueries. This can significantly improve query execution times, especially in cases where the same calculations need to be repeated across large datasets.

Another important role of functions in database design is in enforcing data integrity and consistency. Functions can be used to implement business logic directly within the database, ensuring that data adheres to specific rules and constraints. For example, a function might be used to validate that a phone number meets the required format before it is inserted into the database, or to check that a discount code is valid before applying it to a transaction. This ensures that only valid data is stored in the database, reducing the risk of data anomalies and improving the reliability of the system.

Moreover, functions are often used to implement complex calculations that involve multiple steps. For example, in an e-commerce database, a function can calculate the total price of an order by adding the prices of individual items, applying any discounts, and calculating the tax. By encapsulating this logic in a function, developers can ensure that the calculation is performed correctly every time an order is processed, regardless of where it is invoked. This approach ensures that the logic is centralized, making it easier to maintain and update when necessary.

Functions can also improve the modularity of database design. When logic is encapsulated in functions, the database becomes more organized and manageable. Functions can be treated as building blocks that can be combined to create more complex operations or workflows. For example, a function that calculates the total sales for a particular period can be used in conjunction with other functions, such as those that filter the data by region or product category, to produce a comprehensive sales report. This modularity makes it easier to manage and update the database logic, as developers can work with smaller, isolated components rather than dealing with large, monolithic queries or procedures.

Another key advantage of functions is that they promote reusability. Once a function is defined, it can be reused across multiple queries, stored procedures, or views. This reduces the need to duplicate code and ensures that the same logic is applied consistently throughout the database. This reusability is especially beneficial in large database systems or applications where the same logic may be required in different places. By creating a well-designed library of functions, developers can significantly reduce development time, minimize errors, and simplify the process of maintaining the database system.

However, as with any tool, functions must be used judiciously in database design. While they offer many advantages, overusing functions can lead to performance issues and complexity. For instance, creating overly complex functions or using too many nested function calls can negatively impact the performance of queries, especially when dealing with large datasets. Additionally, because functions are executed within the database, their execution can increase the workload on the database server, potentially leading to slower query execution times if not properly optimized.

Moreover, improper use of functions can lead to difficulties in debugging and maintenance. Functions that are too complex or poorly documented can become difficult to troubleshoot, especially when issues arise in production systems. It is essential for database developers to ensure that functions are well-structured, well-documented, and optimized for performance. Careful consideration should also be given to the scope of the function—whether it is intended for reuse across multiple queries or limited to a specific task—so that the overall complexity of the database does not grow out of control.

Functions are a powerful tool in database design that enhances flexibility, performance, and data integrity. By encapsulating complex logic, automating data transformations, and ensuring consistency, functions play a crucial role in modern database systems. They help developers manage and maintain large datasets, ensure business rules are applied consistently, and optimize the performance of queries. However, careful planning, optimization, and documentation are essential to avoid potential performance issues and ensure that the database remains scalable and maintainable. When used effectively, functions are a key component of a well-designed and efficient relational database.

The Role of Metadata in Relational Databases

Metadata plays a critical role in the functioning and management of relational databases. In simple terms, metadata refers to the "data about data." It provides essential information about the structure, organization, and attributes of data within the database, enabling efficient data management, access, and utilization. Without metadata, understanding how data is stored, related, and accessed would be nearly impossible. Metadata acts as a bridge between users, applications, and the underlying database systems, facilitating operations, ensuring data integrity, and enabling various administrative tasks. The importance of metadata in relational databases cannot be overstated, as it serves as the cornerstone for effective data modeling, query optimization, security, and overall database management.

At its core, metadata in a relational database describes the structure of the database itself, including tables, columns, relationships, indexes, and constraints. This information is typically stored in system tables, which are managed by the database management system (DBMS). These system tables contain data about the database objects, such as the names, data types, and relationships of tables and columns. For example, when a user queries a relational database, the DBMS utilizes the metadata to understand how to retrieve the requested data efficiently. It uses metadata to determine which tables contain the required information, how those tables are related, and which indexes can be used to optimize query performance.

One of the primary functions of metadata in relational databases is to describe the schema of the database. The schema defines the structure of the database, including the tables, their columns, the data types of those columns, and any constraints that apply to the data. This information is vital for understanding how data is organized and accessed. For instance, metadata allows the DBMS to identify whether a column contains numerical values, dates, or text, and whether any constraints, such as uniqueness or foreign key relationships, need to be enforced. Without metadata, it would be impossible to perform operations like joins, data validation, or even basic queries on the database, as the DBMS would lack the context needed to interpret the data correctly.

Additionally, metadata plays a crucial role in ensuring the integrity and consistency of the data stored in a relational database. Constraints are a key component of database integrity, and metadata is used to define and enforce these constraints. For example, the metadata might specify that certain columns must not contain null values or that a foreign key must always reference a valid record in another table. These constraints are automatically enforced by the DBMS based on the metadata, ensuring that the data remains consistent and accurate. Metadata also helps in tracking relationships between tables, which is especially important in relational databases where tables are often interconnected through foreign keys. The metadata ensures that these relationships are properly maintained and prevents the insertion of inconsistent or invalid data.

Metadata also significantly enhances the ability to perform efficient queries and data retrieval. When users or applications request data from the database, the DBMS uses metadata to determine the best way to retrieve the data. This includes deciding which indexes to use, how to join tables, and which columns to return. Indexes, which are part of the metadata, are used to speed up data retrieval by providing quick access paths to data. For example, if a query asks for a list of all orders placed by a specific customer, the metadata will indicate whether there is an index on the customer ID column of the orders table. If such an index exists, the DBMS can use it to quickly locate the relevant orders without having to scan the entire table. Metadata thus improves query performance and makes the database more responsive.

Beyond querying, metadata also plays a role in query optimization. Query optimization is the process by which the DBMS determines the most efficient way to execute a query. The DBMS analyzes the metadata to understand the structure of the tables involved in the query, the relationships between them, and the available indexes. By doing so, the DBMS can rewrite the query to minimize the amount of data that needs to be scanned, use indexes effectively, and reduce the overall execution time. For example, metadata can reveal that certain columns are indexed, allowing the DBMS to choose the fastest possible method for accessing the data. Without accurate and up-to-date metadata, the query optimizer would be unable to make informed decisions, potentially leading to slower query performance.

In addition to improving query performance and enforcing data integrity, metadata also facilitates database administration tasks. Database administrators (DBAs) rely heavily on metadata to monitor the health and performance of the database, perform backups, and ensure that the database is running efficiently. Metadata provides essential insights into the structure and usage of the database, such as which tables are the largest, which indexes are being used most frequently, and which queries are taking the longest to execute. By examining the metadata, DBAs can identify potential performance bottlenecks, optimize indexes, and make adjustments to improve overall database performance. Metadata also helps DBAs manage access control and security by providing information on user privileges, roles, and access rights.

In large and complex databases, metadata can also be used to automate tasks such as data migration, replication, and synchronization. For instance, when migrating data from one database system to another, metadata provides the necessary information to map the structure of the source database to that of the destination database. This includes identifying the tables, columns, and data types that need to be transferred and ensuring that the relationships between the data are maintained. Similarly, in distributed databases, metadata can help synchronize data across multiple nodes by tracking changes and ensuring consistency between the different database copies.

In terms of security, metadata also plays a vital role in auditing and compliance. Many organizations are required to track who has accessed or modified their data, especially when handling sensitive or regulated information. Metadata can be used to log these activities, providing an audit trail that helps organizations comply with legal and regulatory requirements. For example, the metadata can record which users accessed a specific table, what queries they executed, and when these actions took place. This information is invaluable for security audits and helps ensure that any unauthorized access or suspicious activity can be identified and investigated.

While metadata provides numerous benefits, it also introduces challenges in terms of management and maintenance. As the database evolves, the metadata must be kept up-to-date to reflect changes in the schema, indexes, constraints, and other database elements. Inaccurate or outdated metadata can lead to issues such as poor query performance, data integrity problems, and difficulties in maintaining the database. Therefore, it is crucial for database administrators and developers to regularly review and update the metadata, ensuring that it accurately reflects the state of the database.

Metadata is a foundational aspect of relational database design and management. It provides the necessary context for understanding the structure of the data, enforcing integrity constraints, optimizing queries, and performing a wide range of administrative tasks. Metadata not only enhances the performance and efficiency of a database but also helps ensure data consistency, security, and compliance. In modern relational databases, the role of metadata is indispensable, as it facilitates smoother data access, better management, and more informed decision-making. Effective metadata management is crucial for maintaining a well-organized, high-performing, and secure database system.

Data Aggregation and Reporting in Relational Databases

Data aggregation and reporting are crucial aspects of relational databases, enabling organizations to extract meaningful insights from large volumes of data. Aggregation refers to the process of summarizing, grouping, or performing calculations on data, while reporting is the presentation of this aggregated information in a format that is easy to understand and interpret. Together, these processes support decision-making, analysis, and business intelligence by transforming raw data into actionable insights. Relational databases, with their structured data model and SQL querying capabilities, provide the necessary tools to perform aggregation and generate reports efficiently.

In relational databases, data aggregation typically involves operations such as summing values, counting occurrences, calculating averages, finding minimum or maximum values, and performing other mathematical or statistical computations on sets of data. These operations are often used to summarize large datasets and identify trends or patterns. For instance, in a sales database, an aggregation might be used to calculate the total revenue for each product category, the average order size, or the total number of customers over a given time period. SQL's aggregation functions, such as SUM(), COUNT(), AVG(), MIN(), and MAX(), are the core tools for performing these operations, allowing users to group and aggregate data efficiently.

One of the most powerful features of relational databases when it comes to aggregation is the ability to group data based on certain attributes. The SQL GROUP BY clause allows users to group rows of data based on one or more columns and perform aggregation on each group separately. For example, a query might group sales transactions by product category and calculate the total revenue for each category.

Grouping data in this way allows for detailed analysis of subsets of data, enabling organizations to better understand how different segments of their business are performing. The GROUP BY clause is often used in combination with aggregation functions to produce summarized data, such as the total sales for each region or the average salary for each department in a company.

In addition to simple aggregation, relational databases also support more advanced techniques for data analysis and reporting. For example, the HAVING clause can be used in conjunction with GROUP BY to filter groups based on the result of an aggregate function. This is useful when there is a need to only include groups that meet certain criteria, such as selecting only those product categories with total sales greater than a specific threshold. This type of filtering adds another layer of flexibility to data aggregation, allowing users to focus on the most relevant information for their analysis.

Once data has been aggregated, the next step is often reporting, which involves presenting the aggregated data in a meaningful way. Reports are typically formatted for consumption by decision-makers, analysts, or other stakeholders who need to interpret the data and make informed decisions. Relational databases provide a range of tools and features for generating reports, often through SQL queries that can be formatted to meet specific reporting requirements. These reports can range from simple tabular displays of data to more complex visualizations, such as charts and graphs, depending on the needs of the organization.

One common type of report is a summary report, which presents the results of aggregated data in a concise format. For instance, a company might use a summary report to display the total revenue for each month over the past year, along with the average revenue per customer or the highest revenue-generating product category. These reports are typically used by management to get an overview of key business metrics and make strategic decisions. In addition to summary reports, relational databases can also generate detailed reports that include row-level data, such as a list of all sales transactions within a specific time period, or customer-level reports showing individual purchases and spending habits.

Relational databases also support more complex reporting requirements, such as multi-dimensional reporting, which allows for the analysis of data across multiple dimensions. This is particularly useful in business intelligence (BI) applications, where data needs to be analyzed from various perspectives, such as by time, region, product, or customer segment. For example, a sales report might need to show total revenue by both region and product category, with the ability to drill down into more granular levels of detail. Relational databases can support this type of reporting by using techniques such as pivot tables or multidimensional queries, which allow users to view the data from different angles and uncover deeper insights.

In many cases, relational databases can be integrated with third-party reporting tools to enhance reporting capabilities. These tools often provide advanced features such as interactive dashboards, data visualizations, and the ability to create customized reports without writing complex SQL queries. By connecting a relational database to a reporting tool, organizations can automate the process of generating reports and deliver them to users in a more accessible and user-friendly format. These tools can also allow users to schedule regular report generation and distribution, ensuring that decision-makers have timely access to the data they need.

Data aggregation and reporting also play an important role in maintaining data consistency and accuracy. When performing aggregation, it is essential to ensure that the data being summarized is complete and accurate. For example, if a sales report is showing the total revenue for each product category, the database must ensure that all relevant transactions are included in the calculation and that no duplicate or erroneous data is considered. This requires careful data cleaning and validation prior to aggregation, which can be automated within the database through constraints, triggers, and stored procedures.

As the volume of data continues to grow in modern organizations, the need for efficient aggregation and reporting becomes even more critical. Relational databases, with their ability to handle large datasets, provide the necessary infrastructure to process and aggregate this data efficiently. However, as the complexity of the data and the reporting requirements increase, so does the need for careful database design and optimization. Indexing, partitioning, and query optimization are key techniques that can be used to improve the performance of aggregation and reporting queries, ensuring that reports are generated quickly and accurately, even in large and complex databases.

Relational databases also offer features such as materialized views, which can be used to store the results of complex aggregation queries. These precomputed results can be quickly accessed and used in reports, reducing the computational load on the database and improving performance. Materialized views are especially useful for reports that require frequent aggregation of large datasets, as they allow for faster access to the data by eliminating the need to re-run complex queries each time the report is generated.

Ultimately, data aggregation and reporting in relational databases are essential for transforming raw data into valuable insights that support decision-making and business intelligence. Through the use of aggregation functions, advanced querying techniques, and reporting tools, organizations can gain a deeper understanding of their data and make informed decisions that drive business success. Whether for high-level executive reports or detailed operational analysis, relational databases provide the foundation for efficient and effective data aggregation and reporting, enabling organizations to unlock the full potential of their data.

Relational Databases and Big Data: An Integration Approach

The rise of big data has transformed how organizations collect, store, and analyze information. As data sources become increasingly diverse and complex, businesses must adapt to manage and leverage large volumes of structured, semi-structured, and unstructured data. Traditional relational databases, long the backbone of enterprise data management, are now being challenged by the scale and variety of big data. However, rather than competing with each other, relational databases and big data technologies can be integrated to provide a more comprehensive solution. The integration of relational databases with big data frameworks offers a robust approach to managing data, blending the strengths of relational systems with the scalability and flexibility of big data technologies.

Relational databases have been the standard for managing structured data for decades. They organize data into tables with predefined schemas, ensuring data consistency, integrity, and easy retrieval using SQL queries. Relational databases excel at managing transactions, maintaining data integrity through ACID (Atomicity, Consistency, Isolation, Durability) properties, and supporting complex queries on structured data. They are ideal for handling business-critical applications such as inventory management, financial transactions, customer relationship management (CRM), and more. These systems are optimized for performance in scenarios where data relationships are well-defined and consistent.

However, the advent of big data has introduced new challenges. Big data refers to vast datasets that are too large, diverse, or complex to be processed by traditional relational database systems. Big data encompasses not only structured data but also semi-structured and unstructured data, such as text, images, video, social media posts, and sensor data. Big data technologies like Hadoop, Apache Spark, and NoSQL databases were designed to handle the massive volume, velocity, and variety of modern data. They provide horizontal scalability, fault tolerance, and flexibility in processing and analyzing data at scale, making them particularly suitable for tasks such as predictive analytics, machine learning, and real-time processing.

While big data technologies excel at managing large volumes of data and providing insights from diverse data sources, they often lack the transactional integrity and structured query capabilities that relational databases offer. For example, NoSQL databases, commonly used in big data environments, prioritize scalability and flexibility but may sacrifice features like strict consistency and relational querying. This is where the integration of relational databases and big data solutions can create a powerful data architecture.

The integration of relational databases with big data technologies allows organizations to leverage the strengths of both systems. One common integration approach is to use relational databases for operational data management while leveraging big data platforms for advanced analytics and processing. Relational databases can continue to store and manage structured transactional data, ensuring data consistency and integrity, while big data platforms handle unstructured data, large-scale analytics, and real-time data processing. This hybrid approach provides the best of both worlds—relational databases ensure reliability and consistency, while big data technologies enable scalability and flexibility for complex analytical tasks.

One method of integrating relational databases with big data systems is through data warehousing and ETL (Extract, Transform, Load) processes. In this approach, data from relational databases can be extracted, transformed into a suitable format, and loaded into big data platforms for analysis. For example, transactional data stored in relational databases can be transferred to a Hadoop-based data warehouse, where it can be analyzed alongside other large datasets, such as log files, social media feeds, or sensor data. This integration allows organizations to use relational databases for day-to-day operations while enabling data scientists and analysts to perform advanced analytics and gain insights from big data.

Another approach to integration involves using connectors or middleware that enable relational databases to interact directly with big data platforms. For instance, some relational database management systems (RDBMS) have built-in connectors for big data technologies, such as Apache Hadoop, Apache Spark, and cloud-based data lakes. These connectors allow relational databases to push data to big data systems for processing, and then retrieve the results for further analysis. This direct interaction between relational databases and big data systems eliminates the need for a separate ETL process and provides real-time or near real time access to big data insights.

Additionally, integrating relational databases with big data can enable organizations to combine the strengths of SQL with the scalability and processing power of big data systems. Tools like Apache Hive and Apache Impala, which are built on top of Hadoop, allow users to run SQL queries on large datasets stored in Hadoop clusters. These tools provide a familiar interface for database administrators and analysts, enabling them to apply their SQL skills to big data without having to learn new query languages. This integration bridges the gap between the structured data of relational databases and the unstructured or semi-structured data typically handled by big data technologies, allowing organizations to seamlessly query and analyze diverse datasets.

The integration of relational databases with big data technologies also supports real-time data processing and analytics. For example, organizations that use relational databases to manage transactional data can use big data technologies like Apache Kafka and Apache Storm to process streaming data in real time. By integrating these technologies, organizations can track and analyze data as it is generated, enabling real-time decision-making. This is particularly valuable in industries like finance, healthcare, and e-commerce, where being able to respond to data as it arrives can provide a competitive advantage.

Security and data governance are also key considerations when integrating relational databases with big data systems. Relational databases are known for their robust security features, including user authentication, access control, and data encryption. Big data platforms, while scalable and flexible, often require additional considerations for managing access and ensuring data privacy. By integrating the security features of relational databases with the scalability of big data technologies, organizations can ensure that sensitive data is protected while still enabling large-scale analysis. Data governance frameworks can also be applied across both relational and big data systems to ensure that data quality, compliance, and privacy standards are met.

Despite the benefits of integrating relational databases with big data technologies, there are challenges to consider. One of the main challenges is ensuring data consistency across different systems. Relational databases enforce strict consistency through ACID properties, while big data platforms, especially those based on NoSQL, often prioritize availability and partition tolerance over consistency (as per the CAP theorem). To address this, organizations must carefully design their integration processes, ensuring that data synchronization and consistency are maintained across the systems. Additionally, managing the complexity of the integration architecture, ensuring that data flows smoothly between relational and big data systems, and optimizing performance can require careful planning and technical expertise.

The integration of relational databases with big data technologies provides a powerful solution for organizations that need to manage both structured transactional data and large-scale, unstructured data. By combining the reliability and consistency of relational databases with the scalability and processing power of big data systems, organizations can unlock the full potential of their data. This hybrid approach enables real-time analytics, advanced processing, and deeper insights, all while maintaining the integrity and efficiency of relational database systems. As the volume and complexity of data continue to grow, the integration of relational databases with big data technologies will play an increasingly important role in helping organizations stay competitive and make informed decisions based on their data.

Artificial Intelligence and Machine Learning in Relational Databases

The convergence of artificial intelligence (AI) and machine learning (ML) with relational databases is revolutionizing how organizations manage, analyze, and derive insights from their data. Relational databases, long known for their structured data storage and efficient querying capabilities, are now being enhanced with AI and ML techniques to process vast amounts of data, uncover patterns, and make predictive decisions. This integration brings a new level of intelligence to database management, providing automated insights, improved decision-making capabilities, and the ability to process complex data more efficiently.

At the heart of this transformation is the ability to apply machine learning models directly within the database. Machine learning allows databases to move beyond traditional querying and reporting by enabling systems to learn from data, identify trends, and make predictions based on past patterns. In the past, data analysis often required manual intervention, where analysts would build models externally, extract data, and then feed it into these models for processing. With the integration of ML into relational databases, this process is now streamlined, allowing businesses to perform advanced analytics and make real-time predictions directly within the database environment. This not only improves the efficiency of data processing but also reduces the complexity of managing external tools and platforms.

Relational databases have traditionally been used for structured data, such as transactional information stored in tables with well-defined schemas. However, machine learning requires large datasets, including unstructured or semi-structured data, which is often difficult to manage within traditional relational systems. To address this challenge, many modern relational databases are being enhanced with AI and ML capabilities that can handle both structured and unstructured data. These capabilities include tools for natural language processing (NLP), image recognition, and predictive analytics, which allow relational databases to process data types that were once outside their scope. For example, a company could use AI integrated into its relational database to analyze customer reviews (unstructured text data) alongside traditional structured sales data to gain deeper insights into customer sentiment and purchasing behaviors.

One of the most significant applications of AI and ML in relational databases is in predictive analytics. By training machine learning models on historical data stored in a relational database, organizations can forecast future outcomes with greater accuracy. For example, a retail company can use machine learning models to predict future sales trends based on historical transaction data, seasonal patterns, and other relevant variables. These predictions can then be used to optimize inventory management, improve demand forecasting, and drive strategic decisions about product offerings and marketing strategies. Similarly, in the healthcare sector, machine learning models can be used to predict patient outcomes based on historical medical records, enabling early detection of health risks and improving patient care.

Moreover, AI and ML can enhance data integrity and quality within relational databases. Machine learning algorithms can be used to automatically detect anomalies in data, identify errors, and recommend corrective actions. This is particularly useful in large datasets, where manual data validation is time-consuming and prone to errors. For instance, a financial institution could implement AI models to flag fraudulent transactions by learning patterns from historical data and identifying unusual behavior in real-time. This automatic detection and correction of issues not only improves the accuracy of data but also reduces the burden on database administrators and data analysts.

Relational databases are also benefiting from AI-powered automation in the form of query optimization and performance tuning. AI and machine learning algorithms can analyze query patterns and suggest improvements to indexing, storage, and query execution plans. For example, machine learning models can be used to predict the most efficient ways to join tables or to identify which indexes are most useful for a given query workload. This not only enhances query performance but also helps ensure that databases are optimized for real-time decision-making, reducing the time it takes to generate insights from large datasets.

Additionally, AI-driven data mining techniques are allowing relational databases to uncover hidden patterns and relationships within data. Data mining involves the use of statistical and computational algorithms to identify trends, clusters, and outliers in datasets. When integrated with machine learning, data mining can take relational data and transform it into valuable insights that might otherwise go unnoticed. For example, an organization can use data mining techniques to segment customers into distinct groups based on purchasing behavior, helping businesses to target specific market segments with tailored marketing strategies. AI and machine learning allow these insights to be generated automatically, making it easier for businesses to act on them without manual intervention.

Another benefit of integrating AI and ML with relational databases is in the realm of recommendation systems. These systems rely heavily on analyzing large volumes of data to provide personalized recommendations to users. By applying machine learning algorithms within relational databases, organizations can build recommendation engines that use historical data to predict which products, services, or content a user is most likely to engage with. For instance, an e-commerce website might use a recommendation system to suggest products to customers based on their past browsing and purchasing behavior. Similarly, streaming platforms can use recommendation algorithms to suggest movies or shows based on users' viewing history. With AI and ML capabilities embedded directly into the database, these recommendation systems can be integrated into applications with minimal latency, providing real-time suggestions to users.

While the integration of AI and ML into relational databases brings significant advantages, it also presents some challenges. One of the primary concerns is the complexity of implementing and managing machine learning models within a traditional relational database system. Machine learning requires significant computational power, and many relational database systems were not originally designed with this in mind. As a result, integrating AI models into these systems may require additional resources and infrastructure to handle the computational demands. In some cases, organizations may need to offload certain processing tasks to specialized hardware, such as GPUs, or distribute the workload across multiple machines.

Another challenge is ensuring that machine learning models remain up-to-date as data evolves over time. Machine learning models need to be retrained periodically to account for changes in patterns and trends. This retraining process can be complex and time-consuming, particularly in environments with large datasets and frequently changing data. As relational databases evolve to incorporate AI and ML capabilities, organizations will need to establish processes and workflows for maintaining the performance and accuracy of machine learning models over time.

Despite these challenges, the integration of AI and ML in relational databases is a game-changer for businesses that rely on data to make informed decisions. It enables organizations to automate complex tasks, gain deeper insights from their data, and improve operational efficiency. By embedding machine learning capabilities directly within relational databases, companies can process and analyze data in real-time, enhance data accuracy, and predict future outcomes with greater precision. This evolution of relational databases with AI and machine learning capabilities represents a powerful step forward in the ongoing transformation of data management and analytics.

Future Trends in Relational Database Management Systems

Relational Database Management Systems (RDBMS) have been the cornerstone of data storage and management for several decades, providing businesses with a reliable way to organize, retrieve, and manipulate structured data. However, as the volume of data continues to grow and technological advancements push the boundaries of what is possible, the future of RDBMS is poised for transformation. Emerging trends are shaping how databases are designed, deployed, and managed, providing businesses with more powerful tools to handle the increasingly complex data needs of modern applications. From the rise of cloud-native solutions to the integration of artificial intelligence (AI) and machine learning (ML), the next generation of RDBMS will leverage these technologies to offer greater flexibility, scalability, and performance.

One of the most significant trends in the future of RDBMS is the ongoing shift to cloud-based databases. The widespread adoption of cloud computing has fundamentally changed how databases are deployed and managed. Traditionally, relational databases were hosted on-premises, requiring significant hardware investment, manual scaling, and complex management. Cloud databases, on the other hand, offer significant advantages in terms of scalability, flexibility, and cost-efficiency. Major cloud providers, such as Amazon Web Services (AWS), Microsoft Azure, and Google Cloud, now offer fully managed relational database services that handle provisioning, backups, patching, and scaling automatically. This shift enables businesses to focus on their core operations while relying on the cloud provider for database management. As more companies adopt cloud-native architectures, the integration of RDBMS with cloud services will become even more seamless, allowing for hybrid and multi-cloud deployments where data can be distributed and accessed across various cloud environments with minimal friction.

With the rise of cloud-based systems, the future of RDBMS will also see enhanced support for hybrid cloud environments. Businesses are increasingly opting for hybrid cloud strategies to balance the benefits of public cloud scalability with the control and security of on-premises infrastructure. In these environments, RDBMS will need to seamlessly integrate data across both on-premises and cloud-based systems, allowing for fluid data movement and synchronization. This will be particularly valuable for organizations that are transitioning to the cloud in stages, as it ensures continuity and accessibility of their data across multiple platforms. Additionally, hybrid cloud solutions will allow organizations to optimize their data management strategies, selecting the best environment for each application or workload while maintaining centralized data governance.

Another key trend is the continued adoption of distributed relational databases. As the need for high availability, fault tolerance, and horizontal scalability grows, distributed relational databases are becoming more prevalent. Unlike traditional monolithic RDBMS, which store data on a single server or a small set of servers, distributed databases spread data across multiple nodes or geographic locations. This distributed architecture enables better performance, fault tolerance, and redundancy, ensuring that databases can handle high traffic and remain operational even if one or more nodes fail. The trend toward distributed databases will continue as businesses demand greater flexibility and uptime, and the complexity of managing distributed systems becomes more manageable with advances in cloud computing, containerization, and orchestration technologies like Kubernetes.

In parallel with the rise of cloud-native and distributed databases, there is an increasing emphasis on performance optimization in relational databases. One of the challenges of scaling relational databases is managing the performance of complex queries as datasets grow. To address this challenge, RDBMS will continue to evolve with features like advanced query optimization, in-memory processing, and the use of new indexing techniques. For example, memory-optimized tables and in-memory column stores are gaining popularity as they significantly reduce the time it takes to retrieve data. In-memory processing allows relational databases to store data in the server's RAM instead of on disk, resulting in faster data access and improved query performance. As data volumes increase and the demand for real-time analytics grows, RDBMS will integrate more sophisticated caching mechanisms and real-time data processing capabilities to meet the performance requirements of modern applications.

Additionally, artificial intelligence and machine learning are playing an increasingly important role in the future of relational databases. AI and ML are being integrated into RDBMS to automate tasks that traditionally required manual intervention, such as database tuning, query optimization, and anomaly detection. AI-powered query optimization is particularly promising, as it enables the database to learn from usage patterns and optimize queries dynamically, improving performance without the need for human intervention. Furthermore, machine learning algorithms can be used to detect anomalies in data, helping organizations identify potential issues such as data corruption, fraud, or security breaches. This integration of AI and ML into RDBMS will allow databases to become more self-managing, reducing the administrative burden on database administrators and enhancing the overall efficiency of the system.

Another future trend is the increasing use of multi-model databases. Multi-model databases combine the features of multiple database models, such as relational, document, graph, and key-value, into a single database system. This allows organizations to store and process a wide variety of data types within the same database. For example, a multi-model database could store structured transactional data in a relational model, while also managing unstructured or semi-structured data like customer reviews or social media posts in a document store. By supporting multiple models, multi-model databases offer greater flexibility and simplify the management of diverse data sources. As data continues to become more varied and complex, multi-model databases will provide a unified solution that enables organizations to handle different data types without the need for multiple, disparate systems.

In addition to these technological advancements, there will be a growing focus on database security in the future of relational databases. As data privacy regulations like the General Data Protection Regulation (GDPR) and California Consumer Privacy Act (CCPA) continue to evolve, organizations will need to adopt more sophisticated methods for securing data stored in relational databases. This includes implementing encryption, both at rest and in transit, as well as employing advanced access control mechanisms to ensure that only authorized users can access sensitive data. Database security will also benefit from the integration of AI and machine learning, which can be used to detect and respond to security threats in real-time. For example, machine learning algorithms can analyze patterns of database access and automatically flag unusual activity that could indicate a potential breach.

Another significant development in the future of relational databases is the use of serverless computing models. Serverless databases abstract the underlying infrastructure, allowing businesses to focus on data management without worrying about provisioning or scaling servers. With serverless relational databases, organizations only pay for the compute resources they use, reducing costs and increasing efficiency. As serverless technologies continue to mature, relational databases will become even more adaptable, allowing businesses to scale resources up or down dynamically based on usage patterns, all while maintaining performance and reliability.

Finally, the future of relational databases will be influenced by the increasing use of blockchain technology. Blockchain, with its decentralized, immutable ledger, has the potential to enhance the security, transparency, and trustworthiness of relational databases, particularly in applications that require auditing or tracking data changes over time. By integrating blockchain with relational databases, organizations could create more secure and transparent systems for managing data, particularly in industries like finance, healthcare, and supply chain management, where data integrity and traceability are critical.

The future of relational database management systems will be shaped by the ongoing convergence of cloud computing, AI, machine learning, and new database architectures. As relational databases evolve to handle the demands of modern data-driven applications, they will continue to provide businesses with the tools to manage data efficiently while offering greater flexibility, scalability, and performance. The integration of emerging technologies will empower relational databases to address the challenges of big data, real-time analytics, and security, ensuring that they remain a critical component of modern enterprise data management.

Best Practices for Maintaining and Managing Relational Databases

Maintaining and managing relational databases is a complex but crucial task for ensuring that the data remains accessible, accurate, and secure. As organizations increasingly rely on relational databases for business operations, ensuring the reliability, performance, and scalability of these systems is essential. Effective database management not only involves ensuring the physical infrastructure is properly maintained but also includes optimizing performance, managing security, performing regular backups, and ensuring data integrity. These practices help in sustaining the performance of relational databases, keeping them secure, and reducing the risk of system failures or data loss.

One of the most critical aspects of maintaining relational databases is ensuring their performance. Over time, as the amount of data grows, database performance can degrade if not properly managed. Query performance can significantly impact the overall responsiveness of the database and the applications that rely on it. To improve performance, database administrators (DBAs) must regularly monitor and optimize queries. This can be achieved by analyzing execution plans to understand how SQL queries are being processed and identifying inefficiencies such as unnecessary joins or missing indexes. Indexing plays a vital role in improving query performance, allowing the database engine to quickly locate data. However, it is important to regularly review and optimize indexes since outdated or redundant indexes can slow down database performance rather than enhance it.

Another essential aspect of performance optimization is ensuring the database is properly tuned. Database tuning involves adjusting various database parameters such as memory allocation, query cache settings, and connection pooling to optimize performance under varying loads. It also includes regularly checking for long-running queries or transactions that may lock up resources and slow down the system. Furthermore, regularly performing database reorganization tasks, such as defragmenting data files and updating statistics, helps maintain optimal performance levels as the database grows.

Ensuring data integrity is equally important in the management of relational databases. Data integrity refers to the accuracy, consistency, and reliability of data over its lifecycle. The primary mechanism for ensuring data integrity in relational databases is through constraints, such as primary keys, foreign keys, and unique constraints, which enforce rules about data relationships and ensure that data is valid. Integrity constraints prevent the insertion of invalid data, such as duplicate records or records with missing values, which could compromise the quality of the data. Additionally, referential integrity is crucial in relational databases to maintain relationships between different tables. Regular audits should be performed to check for any violations of these constraints, ensuring that the data remains consistent across the system.

One key practice for maintaining data integrity is the use of transactional management with ACID properties (Atomicity, Consistency, Isolation, and Durability). These properties ensure that database transactions are processed reliably. DBAs should ensure that all database transactions are atomic, meaning they are completed entirely or not at all, preventing partial updates that could leave the database in an inconsistent state. Properly managing concurrent transactions also ensures that data remains consistent, and locking mechanisms are applied to avoid conflicts or race conditions.

Data backups are an indispensable part of any database management strategy. The risk of data loss due to hardware failure, software corruption, or human error makes regular backups critical for ensuring business continuity. A robust backup strategy should include full backups, incremental backups, and transaction log backups, ensuring that data can be restored quickly in the event of a disaster. Full backups capture the entire database, while incremental backups capture only the changes made since the last backup, reducing storage requirements and backup time. Transaction log backups capture all the transactions that have occurred since the last backup, allowing the database to be restored to any point in time. A well-designed backup strategy should also include testing the restore process to ensure that backups are usable when needed and to minimize downtime during restoration.

In addition to traditional backup methods, cloud-based backup solutions have become increasingly popular for providing offsite backup storage. Cloud backups offer the advantage of scalability, allowing businesses to store large amounts of data without investing in physical storage infrastructure. These cloud solutions can also be integrated with automated backup systems, ensuring that backups are performed regularly without manual intervention. Cloud storage also provides an added layer of disaster recovery, ensuring that data is protected even in the event of a local hardware failure or data center outage.

Database security is a fundamental consideration for relational database management. As databases store sensitive business data, ensuring their security is critical to protect against unauthorized access, data breaches, and cyberattacks. The first line of defense in securing a database is to implement strong authentication and access control mechanisms. Users should only have access to the data and operations that are necessary for their roles, and permissions should be regularly reviewed to ensure they remain appropriate. Role-based access control (RBAC) can be used to grant access based on job functions, ensuring that users can only perform actions that align with their responsibilities.

Encryption is another key security measure. Data should be encrypted both at rest (when stored on disk) and in transit (when transmitted over networks) to prevent unauthorized access, even in the event of a security breach. Encrypting sensitive data, such as customer information or financial records, adds an additional layer of protection. DBAs should also monitor and log database activity to detect unusual or suspicious behavior. Intrusion detection systems (IDS) can be implemented to flag any unauthorized access attempts or abnormal activity, allowing for quick response and mitigation.

Regular database maintenance tasks are essential for keeping relational databases running smoothly. These tasks include monitoring the health of the database, checking for resource utilization issues such as high CPU or memory usage, and ensuring that the database's storage capacity is not exceeded. Routine maintenance also includes updating database management systems (DBMS) to the latest versions and applying patches to fix security vulnerabilities or bugs. It is important to test these updates in a non-production environment before applying them to live systems to avoid potential disruptions.

Database monitoring tools are also invaluable for maintaining relational databases. These tools provide real-time visibility into the performance and health of the database, alerting administrators to potential issues before they become critical. Metrics such as query response times, connection counts, and disk usage can be monitored to identify performance bottlenecks or hardware limitations. Setting up automated alerts for critical thresholds ensures that DBAs can take prompt action to address issues before they impact business operations.

A robust disaster recovery plan is essential for ensuring business continuity in the event of a database failure. This plan should include not only regular backups but also detailed procedures for restoring databases, recovering from hardware failures, and ensuring minimal downtime during outages. The plan should also include redundancy, where data is replicated across multiple locations to ensure that a secondary copy of the database is available if the primary system fails. Testing the disaster recovery plan regularly ensures that DBAs are familiar with the process and can respond quickly in the event of an emergency.

Maintaining and managing relational databases requires a multi-faceted approach that addresses performance optimization, data integrity, security, backup strategies, and ongoing maintenance. By following best practices such as query optimization, using appropriate constraints, implementing strong security measures, and having a robust backup and disaster recovery strategy, organizations can ensure that their relational databases remain reliable, secure, and efficient. As the demands on relational databases continue to grow, adopting these best practices is crucial to ensuring their continued success in supporting business operations and data-driven decision-making.

www.ingramcontent.com/pod-product-compliance
Lightning Source LLC
LaVergne TN
LVHW022316060326
832902LV00020B/3493